The Cacciotti Method

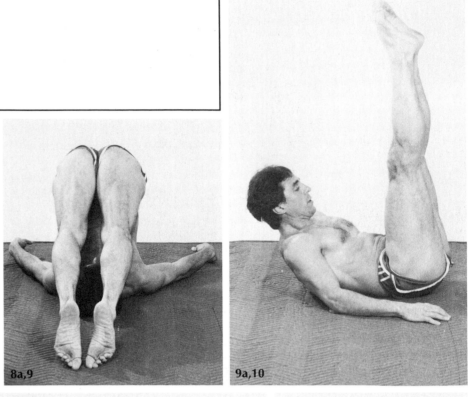

8a,9

9a,10

10a

11

The Cacciotti Method:

The Feel-Good-About-Yourself Workout

Tony Cacciotti

With an Introduction by
Valerie Harper

 VILLARD BOOKS
New York

Book design by Charlotte Staub

Library of Congress Cataloging in Publication Data

Cacciotti, Tony.
  The Cacciotti method.

  1. Physical fitness. 2. Exercise. I. Title.
GV481.C18 1983   613.7'1   82-42802
ISBN 0-394-52567-1

Manufactured in the United States of America
2 3 4 5 6 7 8 9
First Edition

This book is dedicated to all the unfortunate children in the world who, deprived of the very basic substances of life, are not able to experience total health. You, who may never fulfill your potential, take with you the knowledge that we, the privileged and healthy, will never stop until hunger is no longer a problem on this planet.

To the one who
supports my dreams—
"Ti adoro, Valeria."

ACKNOWLEDGMENT

I'm writing this book, which is for people ages five to ninety-five and older, in my office-bungalow at MGM Studios, Culver City, California. Although movement, style, grace, images, perception, emotions and beauty, all ingredients for a successful film, are involved in this book, it is certainly not about motion pictures.

The subject is that classic of all classics, the human body.

Your body, whatever age you may be, male or female. On my fitness chart, middle age is 45 to 65; pre-senior citizen is 65 to 80; senior citizen, 80s to unlimited.

Though I'm currently involved in the production of a movie, my occupation and pre-occupation for many years has been physical fitness and the sculpting of the incredible living form which we all share, uniquely irreplaceable but most certainly repairable.

I wish to express my deepest appreciation to Wernher Krutein, and Roger LeClaire for their fine photographic work. I also wish to thank Leslie Lillien, Ted Therckheld, Evelyn Tosi, Jasmine Gagniel, Leo Kachadourian, Jean Pyatt, and mother and daughter, June and April Tatro, for performing the various stretches and weight lifts. June and Leo are remarkable models in that they are, respectively, seventy and ninety-two years old.

Tony Cacciotti
January, 1983

A special thanks to Ted Taylor,
whose patience and talent
helped shape this book.

A NOTE

The exercises recommend a specific number of repetitions to do, a certain amount of weights to use, a
degree of stretch to obtain, an amount of time to work-out.
These are all *suggestions* and you should modify each
exercise according to *your* own abilities. Do not push your
body beyond its strength — learn to work with your body,
listening to it to know how far to go.

Tony Cacciotti

CONTENTS

EXERCISES

INTRODUCTION

Within the conscious or subconscious of each actress or actor always lurks the question, "How will I look?" If you perform in feature films and imagine yourself on the screen forty or fifty feet high, the answer to that question can be nightmarish.

I think most people ask themselves this question, in different ways, almost every day. And the answer involves much more than just looking good, because good looks on the outside usually indicate good feelings inside. All of us want to feel and look good, but many of us don't do anything about it.

In June, 1979, I was several months away from appearing in Neil Simon's *Chapter Two,* a film in which the camera would rake me over without particular mercy. One scene called for me to wear a bathing suit, and the mirror reminded me of something I'd long known: my hips and thighs were more ample than I preferred. Immediate scaling down was required.

Through a producer friend, I'd heard of Anthony Cacciotti, a physical fitness and body sculpting expert. He was show-business-oriented, having been a Broadway dancer, film stuntman, actor and director. He'd aided such actors as John Travolta, Richard Gere and John Ritter in preparing for film assignments. Quite a few women, including several cancer patients, had benefited from his advice. A number of producers and directors as well as corporate executives in New York and London had also been Cacciotti students.

Urging me to get in touch with my body, Tony taught me an awareness I'd never known, a positive attitude that made me strive and keeps me striving for fitness and beyond that, *wellness*—a true sense of physical and mental health.

I was lucky enough to learn the Cacciotti Method from Tony himself and was also privileged to read this book in manuscript form. To my delight—and happily for you—there is the same wealth of information, quality of advice and enthusiastic support in these pages that I experienced when Tony worked with me personally. His excitement, eagerness and dedication leaps out and will put *you* on the path to greater physical and mental health.

—Valerie Harper

The Cacciotti Method

Better to hunt in fields, for health unbought,
Than fee the doctor for a nauseous draught,
The wise, for cure, on *exercise* depend;
God never made his work for man to mend.
                    John Dryden
                    (1631–1700)

1

WHY NOT A BETTER AND MORE BEAUTIFUL BODY?

Amen!

Stand up and cheer for old John Dryden, an obvious exercise buff. He knew something in the plague-ridden 1600s that we pill-gobbling, space-age inhabitants are just now discovering.

Why pay the doctor (or nowadays a whole team of doctors) or the hospital for cures of one kind or another when good health is essentially available for most people at lifelong bargain-basement prices?

Why not have a better and more beautiful body, male or female? And why not have a longer life in a state of good health?

The positive answer to all these questions lies in a rather simple new approach (though it isn't really new at all) to total health and total fitness, mental as well as physical. It is *wellness* or *well-being,* a self-managed program of proper nutrition, balanced exercise, stress management, adequate relaxation and, perhaps most important, the right attitude, which is *a commitment to be healthy and stay healthy.*

Basic holistic medicine is health management and disease prevention through care for the whole person, body and mind. There is no dualism, no separation of the mind and body. Thus the heel bone is directly connected to the brain cell; the brain cell is linked to the fingernail.

Worth being shouted about from mountaintops, wellness or well-being is even more revolutionary as a preventive medical philosophy because for the first time you assume full responsibility for your own holistic health. The physician becomes an adviser, a teacher, bringing a wealth of experience and knowledge to your own program of health maintenance. A good doctor will freely admit that he or she is not omnipotent; that the patient has a great deal more to contribute to his or her own health than doctors can ever provide. The change in physician/patient relationships is long overdue.

The "keeping well" idea is a revolt against the traditional medical care experience: you are ill, you go to the doctor and he cures you.

Dr. Elliott Dacher, health promotion director of Virginia's Kaiser-Georgetown Community Health Plan's wellness group, considers himself an orthodox physician but tells his patients, "I can't get you well. Everything it takes to get well is already inside each person. It's all there for free, and it can't be purchased. It can only be found in ourselves."

The basic idea of *wellness,* a purely commonsense approach, has been around for centuries, but it was not until the 1970s that holistic health made any substantial inroads into the American medical profession. In 1980 some one hundred wellness centers were established throughout the country. The Swedish Medical Center in Englewood, Colorado, founded the Swedish Wellness Center in 1978 to keep people *out of the hospitals.* So swift was the rise of this health trend that Bristol-Myers sponsored ten wellness hours on USA Cable TV before the end of 1981. Wellness groups and centers are now multiplying monthly.

To those of us who have long worked in physical fitness, and have, indeed, been dedicated to good health, it is gratifying to witness not only doctors but the general public suddenly awakening to the values of birth-to-death wellness. I remember when I began running nearly thirty years ago, people would shout as they drove by, "Get a horse!" It pleases me greatly to now see runners and walkers out in droves.

There are no magic formulas or medical mystiques involved in fitness and wellness. Common sense alone should dictate the approach. Dr. Allan Goldstein, chairman of the biochemistry department of George Washington University Medical School, nationally recognized as an expert on aging, told *50 Plus* magazine: "First, eat wisely and make sure you get enough vitamins, minerals and nutrients. Second, get enough exercise. Third, don't smoke. Fourth, have an active sex life. Fifth, and most crucial, have a positive outlook on life." What applies to the readers of *50 Plus* also applies to the inhabitants of nursery schools and all ages in between.

A 1975 U.S. Public Health Service survey revealed that 51.5 percent of Americans do *no* regular exercise of any kind, and the percentage a decade before was even higher. Little wonder that 850,000 people die yearly from heart attacks.

But one of the sorriest comments on American society today is the number of advertisements in national magazines for teenage fat farms and summer camps to shape up kids between eight and eighteen. Slim 'n' trim down at Camp Lardaway! What kind of life-style have we encouraged? Will we continue to encourage it? I hope not.

Needless to say, healthiness is the body's normal state. The body *wants* to be healthy, but many people seem to have a passive if not negative attitude toward the subject. In fact, body abuse seems to be the favorite American pastime in terms of nutrition. That old fitness-expert complaint that most people take better care of their automobile engines than they do of their own motors happens to be an accurate reflection of the truth.

I firmly believe that you have to want to be healthy and then make a definite commitment to it. It's not enough to say: "I have to walk, jog or run, or I'll die of a heart attack." You have to say: "Hey, walking, jogging or running makes me feel great. It gives me this fantastic energy that carries me through the whole day." You don't have to *like* exercise; rather, once you make it part of your life, you will *love* the results.

How do you attain the physical part of wellness? *You strive for total fitness and are constantly aware of it: as you go about the activities of your life, feel fitness in every muscle; see fitness in your mirror; hear fitness in your voice; breathe fitness in and out every moment of every day.*

Although my special field of expertise is exercise—the physical side of wellness, which walks or runs hand in hand with the mental attitudes—I do know that physical fitness enhances all of your life. A strong and healthy body often leads to strong and healthy relationships with your spouse, children, family members and friends. Strength and health are also the keys to fine-tuning sexual relationships.

By making the decision and commitment to *be* healthy and remain healthy, and by taking your health into your own hands, you'll exercise and strengthen an often overlooked and underused mental process so important to any physical activity—*the will.*

True fitness, as the ancient Greeks knew, is a combination of mind and body. There can be no separation. You must *will* your body to walk, jog or run; *will* your legs and arms to pick up weights; *will* your torso to do ten, fifteen, twenty stretches; *will* yourself to eat proper food; *will* yourself to abstain from smoking, excessive alcohol, drugs.

Stretching exercises increase agility, leading to balance and body control. Walking, jogging and running will increase endurance and benefit the cardiovascular system. Lifting weights—for females as well as males—increases strength and muscle tone. The body and the mind need agility, endurance and strength.

Every time you exercise your will by making a physical decision and sticking to that decision, you become stronger in mind *and* body. What's more, you'll communicate with your body, feel it change; receive responses you never thought possible; establish an awareness in parts and in the whole. Once you become totally healthy and fit, you won't ever want to return to that former neglected self.

Once you decide to commit yourself to good health and total fitness, to the goal of well-being, it won't be necessary for you to have a personal fitness instructor like me. You'll have enough confidence to be your own expert.

A BETTER AND MORE BEAUTIFUL BODY

5

Furthermore, as parents you will serve as good examples in fitness and food awareness, showing love and care to your children that will last a lifetime and be passed along to future generations. The mother and father, or either one separately, who eat rich, fatty foods can expect to raise an unhealthy if not overweight child. The odds are very much against the child being unlike the role model at the table. If the main exercise in the household is walking to or from the car, the parents can more than likely expect to witness the growth of a physically weak and uncoordinated child.

If you look far enough ahead, with people now projected to live well into their seventies and eighties and beyond, no greater contribution can be made to one's children than fitness and health. All the material, intellectual and spiritual contributions mean little if the body must cope with chronic illnesses over a lifetime. Additionally, the bad health of one person affects the lives of all those around them.

Though I'd never heard of role modeling, my own kids were raised watching me work out. I thought nothing of it. They saw me work with weights and eventually lifted weights and ran with me on their own volition, which is the ideal way for it to start. All four boys, three grown, have good bodies and are good athletes. But any role modeling I did was purely without thought. Parents can guide without pushing, and should be highly visible in exercising; be there as support. Food awareness—what is good and what is bad—should be a frequent but casual topic of conversation.

Further, the parent or parents should encourage the child to enter a variety of athletics for many reasons chiefly for the development of coordination and self-assurance. I don't mean *pressure* the child to play any particular sport but *encourage* the child to choose one or more sports. It may be tennis, gymnastics, football, volleyball or any others, but it should be a sport that requires hand and foot and torso coordination. Parental pressure is usually self-defeating. Encouragement is the only way.

In working with children, I've never found the need to design or tailor any specific exercise according to age. Lower age simply means fewer repetitions in the stretches, smaller weights and fewer repetitions in lifting. I would never force a child to do stretches or lift weights. Encouragement by example is the best way.

As with adults, children must especially be supervised when working with weights of any kind. Their tendency is to do more, not less, which could result in injury. Most young children find little fun in lifting weights, and only do it to copy mother or father, and then infrequently. If the child is running, swimming or biking alongside you, common sense dictates that you set the pace for the age, size and stamina of the child.

To me, what is most important is the parental attitude toward fitness and total health. The child may not participate very often, especially up to the teens, but he or she can see the parent striving daily for good and continued health.

And there is no greater gift than a healthy body.

2

BODY SCULPTING:
Could You Show Me How?

I n one way or another, I've been body sculpting since my teens. Though I had no expertise, I remember doing it as a sixteen-year-old exercise instructor at a gymnasium in Miami, Florida, moonlighting from a nearby college prep school. Even earlier, I was lifting weights at the YMCA in my hometown, Auburn, New York.

Other than having a compelling urge, just why I was so much into physical fitness as a kid is still a mystery to me. No other member of my family was involved in acrobatics, running, lifting weights—the latter considered idiotic at the time—or into contact sports of any kind. I was the *rinnegato*, the ragtag family renegade, doing all sorts of strange things.

My parents were from Italy and were dismayed by what I was doing. "Your lessons are what counts," they said. My factory- and construction-worker father was from a village near Rome, and my mother, who spoke no English, was from Abruzzi. They were hard-working immigrants who wanted their fourth son to be a doctor or lawyer, certainly not a football player or, worse, a weight lifter. I once brought home a handsome trophy from a Little League all-star game. They asked, "What are you going to do with that?"— as if it had no value. Nonetheless, they were good parents, aiming toward the sky for me.

But the nearest I ever came to higher education was at a junior college in Mississippi, sent there by the University of Miami, which had scholarship dibs on my legs and shoulders as a running back. The athletic department had hoped to raise my grade average, but a *paisano* from New York, via Pennsylvania and the Hialeah racetrack just didn't fit into the Mississippi mud. I fled.

Somehow I never got off the fitness track. Although I never became the lawyer my parents wanted, I've come to believe that there are no loftier goals than the attainment and the sharing of good physical and mental health. Not for a fraction of a second do I regret the course I took.

So, from hanging upside down in the trees around our house, or entertaining the neighborhood Ukrainian and Polish boys with handstands and other feats, I went on to instruct in and manage musty gyms in Florida, New York and California. Eventually I went into the theater, working in summer stock, off-Broadway and finally Broadway productions. Later on, I acted and did stunt work in films.

No matter what I was doing, or where I was, the road always led back to the gyms—New York, Hollywood, London, Rome or Munich—and "working out" at least five or six times a week. Working out has always been as much a part of my life as eating or sleeping. While dancing in *Jesus Christ Superstar,* I set up a gym in the basement of New York's Shubert Theatre, and the entire cast was soon sweating away with me—the contagious fitness bug bites everyone.

If I did stunts in the daytime in European films, I stretched and pumped iron (lifted weights) in a gym several nights a week. The Romans and Müncheners thought I was crazy when they watched me run my five miles every morning.

During these formative years, someone was always asking, "Tony, could you show me how to . . . ?"

Sure!

One of the great things about people in the health and fitness field, I've found, is our willingness to explain and demonstrate. We feel a need—a burning compulsion—to spread the word that health is beautiful; that improving flexibility, coordination, agility and muscle toning, no matter the age, is always possible.

However, I was also becoming aware of just how many people outside my world of gyms were unhealthy and unfit. Their bodies were off-center and inflexible. Many walked with the grace of a hippo. Most didn't even know how to breathe, and I'd wager that that particular population segment is in the majority, even though oxygen is the fuel that keeps us alive. Babies know how to breathe, but sadly not many adults do.

Out of this realization came what I guess I should finally call the Cacciotti Method, though that sounds imposing, like some new birth control regimen. It's neither imposing nor difficult.

Quite simply, it is a tested program of proper breathing, weight lifting, general stretching exercises for both men and women with some special stretching for women; cardiovascular enhancement through walking, running, swimming, jumping rope or biking, and commonsense food awareness.

With even modest dedication, results are noted within two to three weeks. By the end of six months, all of the stretch exercises should be easily accomplished; muscle flab should have vanished.

In that time frame, most women, depending on the individual, should be lifting between half and three-quarters of their body weight. In addition to improved muscle tone and strength, a new form of self-confidence develops. Most men should be lifting at least half their body weight if not more. End result of this sculpting: good muscle tone, new strength and body awareness.

Also within that time frame, there should be results far beyond the outwardly cosmetic rewards. Balance and body control, structural awareness and realignment of the body will be achieved as part of the physical fitness package.

Among the changes, you'll be discarding some ancient but popular concepts of exercising. Most of us have performed the rapid repetitive movements of push-ups, sit-ups, toe touches and jumping jacks, ever since our grammar and high school days. These exercises are usually performed with momentum, with the assigned parts of the body pushed, flung or thrown toward a target—arms and fingertips thrown toward the toes in sit-ups, for example.

After doing these rapid-repetitive exercises endlessly in grammar school, high school, prep school, college, in the gyms from coast to coast and in Broadway dance studios, I've decided they are of little value. I've replaced them with slow, deliberate and controlled stretches, learning muscle use through experience.

Though I grouse about the flab and puffing of the whole human race, we're on an unparalleled breakthrough in fitness. A decade ago, no one heard of athletic psychologists or doctors specializing in sports or "gait" specialists for runners. Things happened in the body while working out and we didn't know why or what.

A decade ago, I'd never heard of beta endorphins, the chemicals released by the body during a sustained gym session to relieve pain and produce calmness. Now, sports medical science is telling us about the endorphins and other workings inside the body; about the "runner's high."

Fitness psychology? Absolutely.

We often judge not only ourselves but others on how we look at any given moment, the physical attitudes of a few seconds' observation. Our levels of confidence are all too frequently discernible at the same instant. Unfair judgment or not, it is an everyday occurrence and a part of human interaction.

Examine any group of people, women and men, and the ones with assurance usually stand out, whether in bare feet and jeans or in Givenchy and Brooks Brothers. They are the doers, the competent managers of their own lives, if not others'. Their attitudes set them apart. It is evident in their walk, their posture and their eyes. They exude confidence. In all but rare cases, they are physically and mentally fit. Unfortunately, they are in the vast minority, but they stand out because they've taken the trouble and time to change their lives in a physical sense, and the change, quite naturally, is manifested in a mental sense. I do fervently believe in holistic health and wellness. The spirit and mind and body must work together.

In teaching body sculpting to a variety of clients, I've been continually amazed that highly intelligent and talented people in show business or Fortune-500 chairs have only now come face to face with the obvious personal and professional rewards of total physical fitness.

I often ask a new client, "How do you want to look?"

Very few are forthright enough to say, "Beautiful!" Or, "Strong and slim and trim."

Well, I can't create cosmetic facial beauty but I *can* help to create an inner beauty of physical fitness that will radiate to become an outer beauty. As to how slim and trim and how strong, that is definitely up to the client. I can only motivate and show.

In a way readers of this book will become clients, and my first advice is to use the mirror and ask, "Am I in the best possible shape that I can be for my age?"

If you are thirty years old and female, are you reasonably satisfied with your body and skin for *your* age? If you are seventy and male, are you creaking and stiff as ice? Or are you in the best possible shape for age seventy? A man named Ronald Reagan isn't doing so badly in that regard.

From my personal experience in the fitness field, 99.9 percent of those questioned should readily confess, "No, I'm not!" This happens to be the sorry truth, and I seldom make allowances for anyone, including the elderly. In the late 1960s, I often ran alongside Larry Lewis, a banquet waiter at the St. Francis Hotel in San Francisco. He was 103 years old.

My youngest student began at age five.

Speaking of age, I attempt to be my own best selling point for the pluses of physical fitness and body sculpting. I'll be forty-five on my next birthday, but can—and have—passed for early to mid-thirties. And next year I hope to look twenty-nine!

3

BALANCE AND CONTROL:
Can You Stand on Your Toes Without Wobbling All Over the Place?

Some people seem to be agile and graceful from childhood on, blessed with natural body flexibility, gliding through most of life. The majority of us are not given that gift, nor do we attempt to acquire it. We "clump around."

Though I'm the world's greatest optimist where the body is concerned, flowing torso movement—or plain old gracefulness—has to be among the world's toughest subjects to learn. This is particularly true if you're past your teens. Actually, pre-kindergarten is a good time to start; in fact, I know a lady, April Tatro, a model you'll soon meet, who teaches creative movement to three-year-olds.

There is a fun and fitness program in Irvine, California, for infants six weeks to the ancient age of three. Supervised baby exercise is not new, and there is plenty of cuddling and talking in addition to stimulating muscles. In the children's gym at the Irvine Cultural Center there are rocking tubs, tunnel crawls and balance beams; pull-ups on wooden rings for humans all of three months old.

I don't think we were intended to be clumsy, but somehow we've ended up that way, probably due to the machine age. I doubt that early man, pitted against animals for food, fell over his feet too often. There was also a period when mothers attempted to teach daughters to be graceful; when grace was the key element of dancing. Nature's rhythm is evident everywhere, from the

change of seasons and tides to the movements of lower animals, but we've strayed away from it.

However, there is no law saying you cannot teach yourself to be more agile and graceful, and there are ways of reducing adult rigidity. Through body conditioning, certain stretches and certain weight lifts, which I'll describe and illustrate, it is possible to greatly increase agility. But to accomplish those goals requires definite awareness and considerable concentration on torso movement in the beginning weeks.

As the conditioning advances, the body loosens—it's similar to oil being applied to rusty gears—and agility automatically increases. Awareness of that factor, plus the human desire *not* to be awkward—not just to clump around—also takes over, more or less automatically.

For one thing, just by relaxing head to toe you will go a long way toward acquiring suppleness. Common sense will tell you that a body that is tight cannot be supple. A relaxed body is easier material for conditioning. Physical fitness instructors constantly do battle with board-stiff bodies.

Also, a conditioned body in tandem with the *knowledge that your body is indeed trim*—you are willing to show it off—can go another distance. I firmly believe that gracefulness is in the mind as well as the body.

I paid little attention to how I moved until I met Ricki Starr, a wrestler who played the Eastern grappling circuits in the 1950s and 1960s, going up against such fighters as "Gorgeous" George, Antonino Rocco and "Killer" Kowalski. Ricki's gimmick was to enter the ring wearing ballet slippers and acting like a classical dancer. After a couple of pirouettes and a grand plié—

the audience convinced he was a push-over—Starr would "flatten" his opponent. The audience would go crazy. Starr was tough as a dockhand, but could match Mikhail Baryshnikov in grace.

We worked out together, played a lot of handball and ran laps around the reservoir in New York's Central Park. All the while, Ricki kept after me to go to dance classes with him. He was always trying to improve his act, which is what it was. "Just come with me," he said. "What you can do, fine. What you can't, just stand back and watch."

I finally went along to an old beat-up studio, the Showcase, on Eighth Avenue somewhere between Fifty-fifth and Fifty-seventh streets. Looking like a set for the movie *All That Jazz*, it was a combination dance studio and rehearsal hall. Fit, dynamic and bursting with positive energy, Luigi Facciuto taught the jazz dance classes, and most of his students were in Broadway shows. All professionals, they'd sometimes go straight from the Showcase to the theater and curtain time.

That first late afternoon I watched them do about forty-five minutes of stretching exercises before they took even one dance step. What impressed me most was what those male and female dancers could do with their bodies. Their joints seemed to be greased. I thought, Wow, if I could only be that way.

Profiting by what I'd been doing with yoga stretches, I learned how to "jazz walk" and do jazz turns, in the beginners' class. Feeling the rhythm of the music in my body is as important as hearing it. Luigi, of the *bella figura*, often came by to correct and encourage me, and I moved up swiftly over the next six months, going on to intermediate classes. Wanting to work with the best dancers there, simply because I'd be the better dancer for it, I eventually reached the advanced group. Then I branched off into ballet classes and began working on and off Broadway.

Very physical, dancing low to the ground, I moved around like a cat in the road companies of *West Side Story, Gypsy* and other shows. Though I wasn't very good technically, I knew I looked good. And because I had a weight lifter's strength, whenever they needed a male to do an overhead lift or carry with a female, they'd yell for "Tony."

Dancing gave me a fluidity in movement I'd never had before and introduced me to stretching exercises I'd never seen or heard of before Showcase and Luigi's classes. Equally important, it provided discipline and made me aware of the sensitivity needed in working with groups of people in high-energy endeavors.

Except for performers like Fred Astaire, Gene Kelly or Donald O'Connor, male dancers have usually been stereotyped as sissies—that somehow dancing wasn't an appropriate profession for a man.

During one part of my dancing experience I lived off Houston Street in lower Manhattan, and I remember returning to my walk-up after a performance one sweltering summer night. The neighborhood Hispanic kids, twelve to fifteen years old, always seemed to be out in the street playing stickball or kick-the-can. The nearest park was too far away and they preferred the street, anyhow. They were macho—or trying to be. I'd been the same.

This night the whole neighborhood was outside; parents were sitting on the stoops. Six or eight kids were out in front of my place and one of them made a crack about me being gay, since they knew I was a dancer. I said, "All dancers aren't what you think they are. Instead of razzing guys who want to do something kind of different, why don't you guys try it."

Soon they were doing an intricate jazz walk and they realized that it wasn't effeminate. It was a lot more demanding than playing stickball, and also fun. All of a sudden, parents were watching from windows or from the stoops. We had a real *West Side Story* scene going.

Dancing is, and has always been, a superior form of creative action, and is one of the best available forms of exercise. Over the years, social dances such as the Charleston, jitterbug, the twist and some of the current popular dances have, along with a good time, provided a great workout.

After spending more than ten years, off and on, jumping around stages in New York and most major cities, I had no regrets when I called it quits after eight months in the cast of *Jesus Christ Superstar*. My career peaked when I even came away with an award, "Best Buns on Broadway, 1970," a tribute from fellow dancers. Throwing up his hands, my father would have said, *"Eh buffone!" You clown!* But I'll have you know that good buns are one of the first things many women look at in sizing up a male. The reverse is true, too.

A good-looking rear and Broadway aside, I really wanted to instruct body conditioning full-time and had ideas about combining what I'd learned in weight lifting, yoga and dancing into a multilevel but simple conditioning system; one that would be suitable for any age and appropriate for either sex.

In the thirty odd years that I'd been involved in physical fitness, I'd observed a lot of instructors at work in gyms and not one paid much attention to balance and body control, which to me translate into *agility* and *grace*. I believe that *both* should be the ultimate goals of body sculpting, along with *looking* and *feeling fit*—being thoroughly comfortable in one's own body, good tone, added strength and perhaps loss of excess pounds.

I reasoned that if weight lifting and muscle stretching did their respective jobs, accompanied by some attention to food awareness and, above all, the proper mental attitude, there was no reason not to reach all four goals, the degree of agility and grace being entirely up to the person involved.

Size and sex usually have little to do with the capability of becoming agile and graceful. Proof of this are the six-foot-five, 280-pound guards and tackles in football. Many move with only a little less agility than the running backs. Everyone has seen heavy women dance with the grace of a ballerina. Comparatively, large and heavy people can achieve balance and body control as well as those who are small and slim. How much persistence and sweat an individual is willing to apply is the key factor, *not body characteristics*.

I think that loss of balance and body control occurs at an early age, varying from person to person. How we walk, shown by the varying wear on shoe heels and toes, is one early indication that balance and alignment are out of kilter. If the left heel shows marked wear, and the right shows little wear, it is obvious that one part of the body is being used more than another

BALANCE AND CONTROL

and compensation attempts take over. But no doctor I've ever questioned on the matter has been able to tell me exactly why.

I test a new client for balance and body control with the simplest of all measurements: I ask them to stand on their tiptoes. Most people waver back and forth, pivoting around on their toes to maintain their balance. Some cannot stay up on their toes more than ten or fifteen seconds. Most are shocked at their own poor performance, suddenly realizing they can't accomplish this very basic act of balance. They also don't realize they are seldom called upon to go up on their tiptoes without holding on to some object— like an overhead shelf. The supporting muscles aren't capable of balance.

Balance performance, success or failure, tells me a lot about a prospective client. Obviously, he or she has some work to do in the strengthening of the calf and thigh muscles, those underused sinews with off-putting Latin names like *gastrocnecmius* and *rectus femoris*. It is, and has been, a matter of use and unuse. The latter is always the troublemaker.

I'm very much aware that some people have balance and body control problems caused by complicated physical difficulties. That area should be addressed only by a qualified physician; my area is the person whose body is whole in that regard, but neglected in musculature.

Body alignment is equally important. Automobiles are not the only vehicles that go "out of line" for one reason or another. The human body is often found lacking in alignment and all sorts of problems can develop, internally as well as externally, besides unsightly appearance.

Walk down any crowded street in any city and you're apt to see ten different examples of bad posture within a block—bent-over bodies, bodies leaning to either side like the Tower of Pisa, drop-gutted bodies and variations of all three plod listlessly along in a disheartening parade of unnecessary angles. Having seen all examples half-naked in gyms and having worked with many, I'm convinced that most body alignment problems are the result of laziness rather than physical defects.

The penalty of remaining a prisoner in that out-of-line body is undue pressure on certain internal organs and the possibility of "freezing" that posture as the body grows older. It is comparatively easy to attack a stooper or a Pisa leaner or a rounded shoulders in the twenties and thirties age bracket. At sixty, it may be much more difficult but seldom impossible.

I don't trust my eye in attempting to determine if a body is really centered. Doing "puppet and puppeteer" with the client I use my thumbs, running them down the vertebrae as the client slowly bends forward from the waist. Even if I don't think there's an alignment problem, I still feel along the spine, neck down to tailbone. Pockets of tension can be picked up in addition to off-center signs. If there are enough pockets, the body is liable to be rigid even though the person may not outwardly seem tense or rigid.

Tension and rigidity are the natural enemies of balance and grace, and winning the battle over them is a matter of bringing the body up to the levels of fitness it deserves.

4

BREATHING: Suck in Your Stomach and Throw Out Your Chest— the Worst Possible Way to Take a Breath

When Henry Higgins in *My Fair Lady* sings, "You're second nature to me now, like breathing out and breathing in . . ." to Eliza Doolittle, he is being very truthful, whether or not that was the intent of lyricist Alan Lerner. Breathing *is* absolutely the most second-nature function on earth and aside from asthmatics or people who suffer from emphysema, nobody pays much attention to the ins and outs of air. *But the whole human body suffers from shallow, incorrect breathing.*

Oddly enough, few books on physical fitness or athletic training of any sort ever deal with the subject. Even the best books on running do little more than take a glance at the "super gas" that runs the running machine. I find that incredible.

Though it seems ridiculous even to discuss something so routine and basic, air is the fuel for the operation of the entire physical system—lungs, heart, liver, kidneys, stomach, nerve network, brain. Toes to hair follicles, there isn't a millionth of a centimeter of the human body that doesn't depend on the diffusion of oxygen into the bloodstream. That other fuel, food, is secondary in the life chain.

The heart, the body pump, is connected to the lungs by the pulmonary blood vessels, and the inhalation of air causes the whole motor system to operate. Exhalation is the exhaust function, expelling toxic wastes, particularly carbon dioxide.

Oddly enough, few people ever stop to realize that the very first thing and the very last thing we do as humans is breathe. But between the natural "abdominal breathing" of babyhood and that final breath, most of us severely short-change ourselves in the respiratory department.

After we leave the crib and begin sitting and standing, we're inclined to drift into incorrect "chest breathing," or shallow breathing, and our bodies suffer as a result. Yet the medical profession pays little attention to this deficiency. No doctor has ever said to me, "Show me how you breathe." Even with health-care experts, there is that second-nature block—breathing is just something you do.

Yet it is such a remarkable barometer, tied so closely to the emotions and the full range of body expression. Breath shortens during anger; deepens and lengthens during calmness and contentment; sweetens and sours as an indication of states of health. But no matter its intricacy and importance, we mostly ignore it.

For a long time, I was equally guilty. Then on a late summer afternoon in 1959, I was doing my laundry on West Fifty-sixth Street in New York City when a woman I took to be in her early sixties asked, "Do you know anything about yoga?"

I confessed that I didn't. Furthermore, I was frightened of it. Frankly, I thought that it was a mysterious ritual of an Eastern religion somehow mixed up with sedentary exercises. Smelly incense and meditating gurus had never appealed to me. She said, "I teach a class in yoga and need someone to demonstrate the postures."

On that stifling day, I was wearing a T-shirt and gym trunks. I presumed that I qualified, by physical appearance alone, for what she intended.

The money that Rava Devi offered was certainly adequate for one night a week and would augment what I was making for managing a gym in midtown Manhattan. Despite misgivings, I was also a little intrigued as to what yoga was all about. She conducted the class, mainly populated by

people from the stage, ballet and opera, at a studio adjacent to Carnegie Hall, on Fifty-seventh Street.

The first night I attended I discovered why she'd hired me to do the lotus and the plough and shoulder stands and extreme back bends. Though she was still supple for her age, she could no longer twist and turn her body with the ease and grace that she thought would properly demonstrate the exercises. She worked with me, the apprentice, for about six weeks. I'd been doing stretches of one sort or another for years and these new ones were not too difficult, but as the months went by I began slowly to appreciate what she was teaching and why.

As I held the positions, she'd walk around me and explain what was happening—what muscles were involved and all the benefits of that particular exercise. I also began to learn something about yoga itself and realized I'd been very wrong about it.

As far back as the second century B.C. and the yoga sutras of Pantanjali, yogis believed that "life is in the breath" and breathing indeed is the key factor of hatha, or physical yoga. Breath control, or *pranayama,* is used to calm the physical body. I think both concepts are entirely valid.

At first I tended to laugh inwardly at the bell ringing and incense burning that ended each session, which took care of the spiritual and physical side. But then I realized I was learning something totally new and especially valuable–the attention paid to breathing. Suddenly I felt ignorant of my own body.

As an athlete in contact sports, I'd known what would happen when I ran out of breath from sheer exertion—panting and trying to suck air down into my lungs. I'd "spent" the air and the body would have to stop for a while.

As a runner, I'd experienced "highs" at a time when they weren't discussed, as if I were drunk or had found some secret narcotic. As a weight lifter, I'd used an extra breath to pump up extra iron. All of these things were as well known to me as my left foot. Yet I discovered in that yoga class that I really didn't know how to breathe properly. I'd been shallow breathing for years.

With shallow or "high" breathing, chest or rib cage breathing—all the same thing—only the upper part of the lungs fills with air. It is a constant procedure, unfortunately, for most people. What I call *Total Breathing* fills both the lower and upper parts, and the chest cavity from the diaphragm to the breastbone. On the inhale, *the lower part of the lungs fills first.* On the exhale, the inside of your navel should touch your backbone, figuratively.

In childhood, we're often taught "Suck in your stomach and throw out your chest," the way the U.S. Marines do it. That may be fine for a show on a parade ground, but as a method of breathing it is completely wrong.

"Take a deep breath" is usually understood to mean "expand your chest as much as possible." However, the correct advice would be, *fill your lungs as much as possible; forget about making a barrel of your chest. Extend your navel to the fullest on the inhale. Don't suck it in.*

Females, with smaller chest cavities than males, should practice total breathing for that very reason: the intake area is smaller. Pregnant women, in particular, should practice Total Breathing as an overall health aid.

While there are other advanced yoga breathing exercises, such as "charged breathing" and "alternate nostril breathing"—both very beneficial and each with a definite purpose—I'll stick to Total Breathing, the basis for all hatha exercises.

Often, it is difficult for most people to comprehend what an instructor is trying to convey when teaching breathing, and sometimes I use a balloon to make the point: the usual purpose in blowing into a balloon is not just to fill the neck of it; similarly, the purpose of inhaling air into your body is not just to fill the upper lungs, expanding only the chest. By doing so, you take in two-thirds less air than you should be inhaling, robbing yourself of oxygen. The body was designed and the diaphragm and lungs were constructed for full inhalation.

To a new client, I've often said, "Breathe for me," and the reaction is invariably a frown. *Is this guy crazy? I'm paying him to watch me breathe?*

Most fail the test. I can see their shoulders lifting as they lock air into their upper chest, allowing very little of it to go down into the diaphragm area. The gut sucks in at exactly the wrong time.

The next step for the new—and bewildered—client is a simple demonstration, a do-what-I-do of proper breathing:

Lie down. Totally relax your body for a moment. Now put your fingers on your belly, touching around each side of the navel. Inhale through your nostrils, making sure your stomach fully distends. Your navel should be popping out. Hold the breath a moment. Now exhale very slowly and completely. In an imaginary sense, the inside of your navel should now be touching your backbone.

In this prone position, you can best feel the mechanics of proper breathing. Of course, this happens to be exactly the way a baby breathes before bad habits set in. Nature's way is to extend the diaphragm, that sheaf of muscle between the chest cavity and abdomen; literally pushing against the forward wall of the stomach. In doing so, the lower lungs will automatically fill.

Retraining yourself to breathe properly includes a few sets of inhale-exhale exercises six or eight times a day. "Oh, Jeez," the client says, "that'll take too much time."

Not true! Number 1, you have to breathe anyway; the exercises are simply an extension of what you're already doing. Number 2, all the sets can be accomplished within *five minutes*. Standing or sitting erect, they can be accomplished at home, at work and even while driving a car. The results are instant. Total breathing rejuvenates the body in countless ways.

First, I use a one-two-three count on a slow inhale. One: pushing forward on the front wall of the abdomen. Two: filling the middle of the lungs. Three: finally filling the upper portion; then exhaling on a slow three count. I use only the nostrils, which filter the air through the hair follicles. I recommend that new clients attempt to make a mental picture of the process: the air filling the basement, then the second story, finally the upper floor.

When comfortable with this process, I increase the count to four, taking in more air and holding it for three or four seconds before the slow release.

Gradually, I increase the count up to twelve, taking air in slowly and frugally; then letting it out the same way, controlling it.

The added oxygen begins to show up cosmetically on the surface of the skin with a glowing patina. All of the body functions will respond and brighten. Oxygen stimulates the brain cells, and I firmly believe that most people who breathe properly think more clearly than the ones who are air-starved.

I've often told clients, "Become aware of your breathing. Do it slowly and think about it." Sometimes they've looked at me in bewilderment, particularly the busy-busy corporate types. *Become aware of my breathing?*

Yes, it is not only life-giving, but life-saving, lengthening the days on earth through increased vitality; resisting illness through its cleansing powers.

Unfortunately, Total Breathing cannot be achieved and become your natural way of breathing overnight. The procedure must be practiced three or four times a day to break away from the old habit of shallow breathing. Usually, within a month or two the new way of breathing begins to take over. You are suddenly aware that you are breathing properly without doing it as a specific exercise.

I also know, from personal experience, that breathing, acting as an "overdrive," can help you go beyond that "nth barrier" in doing stretching exercises, providing a final burst of energy to achieve what might have been impossible only the day before. Timing and a positive attitude are also involved here. You gear up mentally and then, with a total breath as the physical trigger, reach the goal. This is pure yoga, and it works.

Breathing and timing can help you stretch an inch or more in many of the exercises which we'll be doing later on. The same applies to weight lifting. I've estimated that a breath can give me as much as thirty pounds or more pumping power when lifting heavy weights.

The idea of breath control to summon strength is continually ridiculed—until it's tried. In 1971, I was acting in and coordinating some special scenes

for *The Longest Yard,* starring Burt Reynolds. We were filming at a maximum security prison at Reidsville, Georgia, with about ten weeks of work to do.

On arriving there, knowing that I wasn't going to be all that busy every day, I asked the warden if I could teach a yoga class to the prisoners. "Are you kidding? No one will be interested," he said. I don't think he knew what yoga was.

So I talked to the guards. They said, "Well, we'll talk to the guys." The guards contacted me a day or two later to say, "They're not interested."

Well, I had tried.

A few days later, Robert Aldrich, the director of the film, asked me to set up a "working out" scene involving the prisoners. So I borrowed a pickup and loaded it with Olympic bars and weights, benches, medicine balls, jump ropes—general gym equipment. Ten or twelve prisoners were to be in the scene in one way or another.

While I was readying it for rehearsal, inmates began drifting toward the nearby fence to watch. A crew member saw them and said, "Hey, Tony, lift some weights. Show these guys."

"Naw." I played reluctant. I wanted him to ask me again.

"C'mon. Show 'em."

So I put some weight on an Olympic bar and started to lift.

"Do some heavy weights."

By now, about a hundred people were watching. Jocks, cast, inmates, guards, film crew. "I'll lift two-eighty," I said. Up it went!

One hulking prisoner said, "How did you do that?" He knew I didn't weigh half of two-eighty.

"Yoga," I answered.

"What the hell is that?" another prisoner asked.

"I don't have time to explain," I said, "but I'll teach you if you're interested."

For the next six weeks, I taught yoga stretches and breath control at Reidsville Prison to thirty maximum security inmates. After the first hour, not one ridiculed the ancient discipline.

Just as we haven't even begun to explore the potentials of the mind, I'm convinced there is a lot we can learn about coupling mental power with breath control, though the yogis have been practicing it for more than twenty centuries. We know that breathing can be used as a tranquilizer; we know that gurus can almost suspend their breathing for a period of time, causing speculation as to possible medical applications.

A set of Total Breathing exercises, prior to either lifting weights or going into stretching routines, are the perfect conditioners, physically and mentally. They help to achieve tranquillity and, later, concentration. The yogis also long ago learned that breath control could be used to deal with temper and anger, suppressing tension; cooling rage and passion. Stress can also be handled or reduced with nothing more than slow, rhythmic sets of total breaths.

I'm inclined to be an on-the-go person. I usually thrive on working long hours at full throttle. But when I need to unwind and come off the track, I find I can sustain a sense of peace by some simple breathing exercises. When I consciously use breathing for the purpose of stress management, I lose all sense of urgency, competition, ambition. Good for body and soul! This is, of course, more application of yoga.

Periodically, every human comes up against a sudden moment of extraordinary stress—perhaps a near miss in a car or a rung breaks from a ladder when you're twenty feet up or a riptide carries you away from the beach or your child is grazed by a speeding truck, and in split seconds the mind and body responds, sometimes dangerously. *The heart roars, the mind seems to spin; there may even be hyperventilation.*

I've had the feeling several times—once, when I rolled a Ford at fifty miles an hour, ending up in a ditch. My God, I thought, my heart will never stop pounding.

Then I discovered a yoga-like procedure that works, which I call Overall Stretch and Relaxer: if you're outside, find a pole or a parking meter; inside, a doorknob will do. For that matter, anything stationary that you can grasp with both hands will serve the purpose. Grasp whatever it is, and plant your feet, lean back slightly and slowly lower your body into a squat, inhaling and exhaling with total breaths, making an extra effort to extend the belly button.

While in the squatting position, still clinging to the pole or doorknob, take another three breaths and then put your head down and totally relax. Count to ten and slowly return to the starting position. If normal breathing and normal heart action has not returned, repeat the procedure. One cycle is usually enough. This is not only good for releasing tension but it is also an excellent stretch for the lower back.

When I was first introduced to yoga, I thought that the only way to meditate was to sit under a pomegranate tree and ignore the fly on the end of my nose. The gurus did it that way, I thought. Then I learned that what I'd been doing, now and then, as a runner, a stretcher, a biker, a rope jumper and a weight lifter—just letting my mind drift—was, in fact, meditating. I didn't need the pomegranate tree or the fly.

The idea that you absolutely must sit stock-still in the lotus position and close your eyes to acquire the peace of meditation is another of those misconceptions about yoga that I had. The stone statue position is only *one* way to achieve a meditation state.

The euphoria that is known as "runner's high" is, to me, a perfect stage for meditation. You are running along in the fresh, cool early morning, arms and legs pumping, sweat flowing, a smoothly oiled rhythm at work, and suddenly something happens inside your head and body simultaneously. Mind

and body function as one. There is a feeling of great peace and contentment; all is well with the world.

The current scientific explanation for that involves endorphins, the proteins released by the brain and pituitary gland during hard exercise. A study conducted by Dr. Daniel Carr and other researchers at Massachusetts General Hospital in Boston indicates these miraculous chemicals are just beginning to be understood. As natural painkillers and body sedatives, it is reasonable that they can bring about meditative states.

But "running highs" aren't really needed to let the mind drift. I think many forms of physical exercise provide the opportunity to give the mind some time for relaxation while the body performs as if programmed.

I've meditated while pedaling along a road or while stretching or lifting weights, letting the physical exertion vanish; finally unaware of it for many minutes.

Except in a physical sense, exercising should never be a matter of stress, and an attempt should be made to clear the mind of all stress factors during the exercise period. They can be tackled later on with a better chance of a solution.

I'm fully convinced that tension can be self-released without need of pills, and in working with high-stress clients, I've seen it vanquished time and time again. After the client has worked out vigorously, I'll suggest that he or she lie flat on the carpet or pad, shoes and socks off; gym trunks slipped down if they bind.

And relax!

I turn the lights down and suggest they start total breaths, eyes closed.

Then I have them mentally address each part of the body, or if they choose, vocally, doing it slowly, softly:

"I feel the tension leaving. . . ."

The toes, each one individually; then the balls of the feet; the soles; the ankles.

Next the calves, knees and thighs.

Then the sexual organ and buttocks.

"I'm drawing a mental line around my stomach. All tension has left it. . . ."

The therapy continues upward through the chest cavity and into the shoulders; then each arm and the hands, the palms and fingers, individually.

On to the head and scalp; the features of the face.

"I feel the tension leaving my eyes. . . ."

The nose, the cheekbones; the mouth and lips.

"I'm drawing a mental line around my head, all tension has left it. . . ."

You may find yourself floating with relaxation before you reach your thighs.

5

STRETCHING:
Anytime, Anywhere, Anyone

S it-ups are the most boring exercises a human can do, mostly a waste of time, and potentially dangerous, in my opinion. I'll also include push-ups and toe-touching, to name some other mossy exercises that date back to army training manuals of the 1800s.

Truly, sit-ups are like eating peanuts. You start with a few and suddenly you're involved with dozens; then hundreds. Insanity may follow. There's no end to them and no need for them.

Over the years, in gyms across the country, I've watched people working out, doing rep after rep: fifty sit-ups, fifty push-ups, thirty leg lifts, thirty touch-the-toes. Every drop of sweat was yelling, "I'm bored."

I usually bit my tongue to keep from saying, "You're also wasting your time. And maybe damaging your back." Occasionally I did say it, and you'd have thought I was cursing motherhood. Too bad, because I think more people stay away from physical conditioning because of boredom rather than because of muscle soreness.

Basically, I'm no fan of sit-ups because I've witnessed back problems that could be traced directly to the simple act of touching toes while seated on the rear end. Be warned that *unless the knees are bent,* sit-ups can give you a lifelong problem. The lower back was not made for that type of jarring. You can usually get away with it early in life, but be on guard past the thirties. If you can't resist sit-ups, then please bend the knees. But there are other and better ways, as will be illustrated, to tone the midsection.

Unless the intention is body building, push-ups are largely a waste of time, though there is relatively little danger in pumping up and down on your arms. If you pump enough, you will, eventually, distort the upper arms and find bulges building in the biceps, shoulders and neck.

I've always believed that many people cling to these ancient, standard exercises because the mindless repetitions have a psychological effect: *doing the same thing fifty times must be helping me.* Mentally more than physically, I think. Just because an exercise is ages old doesn't necessarily mean it is good for everyone.

I think the best answer to the boredom and danger in exercising is the common, equally old, ordinary procedure of stretching. It offers variety, head-to-toe selection of muscles to be stretched and results without dozens of reps.

Among the many lessons we could learn from cats and dogs, one is the fine art of stretching. Rising from a long sleep, they'll often stretch luxuriously, awakening muscles that have stiffened. They certainly didn't read about it in fitness books. Nature told them to do it.

It's a shame that human creatures don't similarly listen to nature and stretch regularly to keep muscles and joints lubricated. This do-it-anytime-anywhere stretching is by far the most superior form of all-around exercise available. It encompasses almost every noncardiovascular exercise known to man or beast, requiring no equipment, no skill and relatively little time.

You can stretch from the forehead and jaw muscles down to the toes in a supine, sitting or standing up position. In fact, making faces in the mirror in the morning—stretching your mouth, jaws; elevating your eyebrows; exercising your eye muscles and sticking out your tongue several times—are very valid stretching exercises. All of this awakens your facial muscles and might even cause you to laugh at yourself. There's no better way to start the day.

Astronauts stretch while suited up. A whole stretching routine can be accomplished while flat in bed. Swimming pools are perfect stretch environments for medical patients with ambulatory problems. The applications are

are almost endless. I know an airline pilot who manages thirty minutes of stretches en route to New York from Los Angeles, never leaving the flight deck. I've taught corporate executives to devote twenty minutes during the working day to stretches while at their desk, often during phone conversations or while dictating.

The kitchen, frequently occupied by mothers, working or not, with its waist-high counters, is a fine place for certain sets of muscle stretches. But any room in the house will serve, as will any space outdoors. Name a space and I can match it with a stretch exercise.

I once asked a client, "How many times do you put your arms over your head each day?"

He laughed.

I said, "I'm very serious. How often do you stretch your arms above your head?"

He said, "Well, I put my shirt on every day," and then fell silent, suddenly realizing that days might go by without his ever reaching upward.·

It is really appalling that millions of older people cannot raise their arms above their heads without difficulty. Some just cannot do it. Unfortunately, that condition starts much younger in our machine/computer age. I have an idea that from forty on, most people seldom exercise the deltoid area, the top of the shoulders. Yet a very easy rotational stretch exercise a few minutes each day will keep that area alive and lubricated.

I had a sixty-five-year-old lady say, "My God, what's happening? I'm having trouble getting things off a high shelf, just reaching."

I answered, "Your own fault! You're not lubricated. Your shoulders and deltoids have tightened up from lack of use!" I put her on stretch exercises, head to toe. Age was never much of an excuse. Not to me, anyway.

By keeping the body alive, you aren't likely to pinch nerves, nor will you develop those tension pockets that are so destructive. Toned and lubricated muscles are strong barriers against geriatric problems.

While stretching is certainly not the answer to everything in physical

conditioning, it goes a long way to answering problems in most areas of the body and there's absolutely no fear of gaining unwanted muscles. Combined with weight lifting, it is certainly my answer to fat, flab and sluggish flesh, and to the body imprisoned by neglect.

Though it is only a catchword, I very much dislike the use of *cosmetic* as applied to body conditioning. It infers that appearance is paramount rather than health. However, it is true that the body will look better after a varied stretching routine. In that regard, exercising does have a definite cosmetic effect.

Indeed, stretching is so versatile that it can actually make short people look taller, simply from posture improvement. If adult and fully grown, short people will not be a half inch taller unless they visit a medieval rack. They will, however, *look that way*. By stretching, body alignment can be accomplished that will render a visually taller, leaner form. But five-five *will be* five-five!

Good posture is only one of the many bonuses of a varied and vigorous stretching routine. Toning up the entire musculature will obviously cause positive body response over the entire torso, the head remaining erect instead of bending; shoulders coming into line and pulling back. The body prefers to be straight, just as it prefers to breath correctly. It simply needs help from its owner.

While the stretch exercises ahead of you begin on an easy-to-do level, they admittedly become more difficult later on. Of course, that is also when the real fun begins—the taxing of the muscles, the infamous "muscle burn."

The "burn" is a gym term describing the sensation felt on an isolated muscle, or grouping of muscles, as the result of a particular exercise, or as the end result of a group of exercises—aerobics, lifting weights, squats, etc. I've been "burned" thousands of times and would generally agree with the description of feeling "on fire," or "hot," or "burning" in a particular area of the body. In my experience, muscle burn occurs from going way beyond the normal amount of repetitions or from holding one position for an extended length of time.

In doing exercises, some people feel they should work toward muscle burn; the hotter it feels, the more accomplishment they feel. It becomes a goal and as long as the exerciser doesn't go to exhaustion just to achieve the burn, it is relatively harmless.

6

PROGRESSIVE MUSCLE RESISTANCE:
Also Known as Weight Lifting

At long last, weight training for everyone—men, women and children in all shapes and sizes and ages and occupations—is being accepted on a worldwide basis. You don't need to be a New York Jet tackle or an Olympic swimmer or a Hollywood film star to benefit from barbells and dumbbells. Physical fitness experts, athletic coaches and medical doctors have done quite an about-face over the past decade and many are now encouraging this simple mode of muscle resistance exercise.

For years, the medical community, for the most part, put down weight training as potentially dangerous. Doctors pointed out the stupidity of being muscle-bound; of risking hernias or other damage to the body. Women were warned they'd end up looking like Mr. America.

But now, because of guidance from sports medical specialists and physical therapists, physicians are rapidly changing their minds and many are lifting weights themselves. Athletic trainers who opposed weight training ten or fifteen years ago now supervise it routinely at almost every university in the country. Weight training is now prescribed for every sport, from baseball to track to tennis.

Experts such as Dr. Eric Hughes, professor of physical education at the University of Washington, claim that weight training is a "must" for the modern athletic training program.

Eugene Inagaki, physical therapist for famed sports specialist Dr. Frank Jobe of the Southwestern Orthopedic Group in Inglewood, California, flatly states that weight lifting is "beneficial for everyone, female as well as male"—except those people who are disabled for one reason or another. In some cases, weights are used in therapy treatment for the temporarily disabled.

This does not mean that weight training has been universally accepted. There are still a number of athletic coaches and doctors who are highly critical, claiming the results are only cosmetic and the possibilities of injury are always present. The former is simply not true and the latter may be applied equally to any form of exercise or sport. If done *properly,* there is no more risk in weight lifting than there is in aerobics, stretching or any other form of calisthenics.

Without the slightest hesitation, I've worked weights with a number of medical patients, including one with Parkinson's disease. Their physicians would not have recommended—or agreed to—weight training had they believed that injury might result. Quite the opposite occurred. Improvement was noted in the patients, including the Parkinson's case. Of course, what may have kept weight lifting in a conditioning closet for almost a century were the big muscle men with puffed biceps on oiled torsos.

But the full beauty of modern weight training is for everyone, with its simplicity and its special selectivity. You can select the parts of the body to be conditioned and strengthened, which is exactly what has made weight lifting ideal for athletes. A budding Chris Evert Lloyd and John McEnroe need to strengthen their hands, forearms, biceps and deltoids. No other exercise offers such a specific avenue to address weak or unused muscles.

**PROGRESSIVE
MUSCLE RESISTANCE**

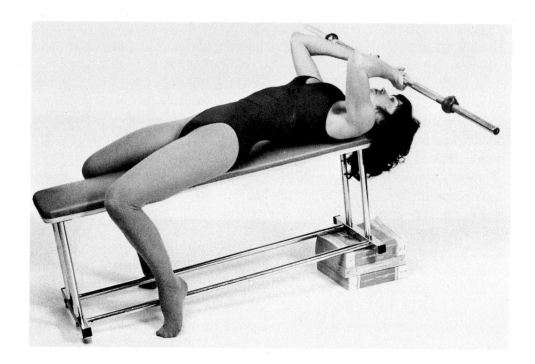

The options for change and development are numerous simply because beneath the skin of most human beings are muscles that are seldom used. Believe it or not, they await *use* and toning.

Rubber bands or elastic tapes grow weaker with use but nature devised muscle fibers to react just the opposite. If resistance, in the form of weights, is added to the normal uses of the muscles, strength is increased. As weight is increased progressively, strength increases progressively. On a selective basis, and by using heavier and heavier weights to impose the resistance, the muscle will also become larger, if that is desired. The lifter is in total control.

Unlike other forms of conditioning, visible and invisible results can be obtained in as little as six weeks. By the end of six months, huge gains in strength can be noted if the weight lifter is willing to work out several times a week, using progressively heavier loads on barbells.

If the particular weight lifter, male or female, wants to look like Hercules and move around like Frankenstein, he or she can work out every single day, five to six hours per session; take steroids and male hormones. He or she will then acquire hill-and-valley muscles.

Or the weight lifter can be selective and just build those muscles that fulfill a definite purpose. The female lifter may be interested mostly in tightening her derriere, shedding the wings and saddlebags that develop on the upper thighs and buttocks.

Maurice "Mo" Williams, six-foot-six star forward for the University of Southern California's 1982 basketball team, finally turned to weight lifting for stamina. All through high school and his early college career, he'd been afraid of weights.

He told Los Angeles *Times* sportswriter Mal Florence, "I believed in the myth that weight lifting hurts your coordination. But there are different types of programs. I didn't want bulk—just strength. You can come out like gangbusters in the first half, but the legs sometimes go in the second half. Also, I wanted more upper-body strength for rebounding and shooting. If you're stronger physically, you're also stronger mentally."

Or there is that average person who wants all-around body conditioning, and wants some cosmetic results as well as strength gain, but certainly not the swells of a contest-winning body builder.

Karen Anderegg, writing about "The New American Body" in the April, 1981, issue of *Vogue*, said, "Working with weights, you can spot-tone, reproportion, build muscle, build strength. You can also—like many women who jog or run or exercise regularly—build new energy."

For example, some women would like to enlarge thin calves that they now hide in slacks. That option exists, through weight training.

Other women are entirely satisfied with their calves, but look higher up the body to the neck and shoulders. The neckline grieves them; they have the option of improving it.

Women can tone their arms. Many women, especially older ones, develop flab in the upper arm and often became masters at camouflage, buying dresses that hide the hanging flesh. Weights and resistance are the only cure that I know for sagging flesh.

But some beginning clients have said, "Well, I'm not so sure about those weights. I don't want to look grotesque."

The fear is certainly ingrained.

"Women still fear muscle definition," Tracey McCullough, instructor at New York City's Sports Training Institute, said in *Vogue*. "What women should realize is that they can control the way their muscles develop. Muscle strength can be achieved without building bulk. With proper instruction, what you can get from resistance training is shapely, toned, attractive muscles."

Debbie Pascuzzi, sports psychologist and visiting professor at the University of California at Los Angeles, points out another aspect to muscle resistance training for women. "Free weights are still a male only domain. There's clearly a social stigma to overcome. The Universal machine is more accepted for women." I think the stigma will be overcome.

Film star Bo Derek is a very attractive advertisement for weight training. She pumps iron regularly.

I explain, in detail, especially to women, that those who want to look huge and muscular have to work constantly at it and do all sorts of special things. The average person will gain muscle tone and strength, but have no bulging biceps, triceps or trapeziuses. The chemistry of the female body is such that chances of excessive, ugly muscle growth are nil. With my program, women can firm up muscles in specific parts of the body; activate others that were dormant, especially support muscles, and generally build strength.

Fortunately there are many kinds of weight training exercises for many purposes and they can be carried out with different sizes of weights. More

than in any other type of physical conditioning, the results can be dictated by the person involved.

A modern gym machine, such as the Nautilus or Universal, lifts within a form. If you are sitting down and pressing, pushing the weight up, the machine doesn't go a quarter inch out of line. It is much easier for an instructor to sit a student down at a machine that is locked in its frame and say, "Okay, do it five or six times." Provided the machine weights are proper for the strength of the student, there's nothing to it.

My objection to the machines is that you cannot become attuned to the particular exercise you're doing; you cannot fully "feel" the weight. I also think that boredom is a greater possibility while working with machines. They depersonalize weight training.

For me, barbells and dumbbells—free weights, those not attached to stationary frames or machines—are the basic, standard pieces of equipment for weight training. Machines are not needed. For home use, weights can be purchased at any sporting goods store or department store. They can also be found second-hand at garage sales and swap meets. Gyms, of course, have elaborate setups for weight training, with multiple sets of weight lifting equipment available.

The "bar" sections of modern barbells are of varying lengths and are adjustable for loading the weights. An inside collar, with a set screw, controls the inward position of the iron or semi-steel disks or plates; the outside collar, also with a locking screw, prevents the weights from sliding off the ends of the bar.

Modern barbells are usually equipped with a sleeve, a hollow pipe that fits over the bar as a hand grip, allowing the bar to rotate as hand positions change. Older barbells, without this feature, are apt to produce blisters and sore wrists.

Barbell plates or disks range from one-and-a-quarter pounds up to one hundred pounds, the latter used mainly by experienced weight lifters. Though iron disks are still the favorites of most weight lifters, many plates now on the market are made of concrete or molded sand, covered with a heavy vinyl. The advantage of vinyl is quietness, plus less wear and tear on floors. Iron disks do scratch, mar and gouge. Most gyms have a variety of barbells, with

fixed weights, and the lifter can select an exact weight off a rack, eliminating time spent to take off or put on the weights.

Dumbbells—fixed or adjustable—are shorter versions of the barbell. Weights begin at a few pounds and increase in five-pound increments up to a hundred pounds or more. For my purposes, they are used for specific standing or incline/decline exercises performed on a bench.

Beginners should buy a barbell set with the total weight of disks adding up to no more than a hundred pounds, either vinyl or iron. I'd recommend trying a second-hand purchase. Would-be lifters often buy a set, work with them for a month, and then the weights sit in the garage. I've seen them advertised for as low as twenty dollars. Dumbbells are even cheaper second-hand. They are often sold as a set, along with the barbells.

Completing the basic equipment is a training bench, a padded light-weight back-and-body support used in certain lifts. These can be bought from sporting goods or department stores for under fifty dollars; second-hand benches go for half that, usually. Or you can make one using wood, though the cost is about equal to the store-bought variety. A pad is required.

One excellent way to acquire the basic equipment is to advertise in shoppers' or *Pennysaver*-type publications, specifying what you need. Those would-be lifters are usually happy to unload. Also you can check the classified ads for bargains.

Dropping a barbell or dumbbell is not unknown, and I suggest that tennis shoes or gym shoes, with good arch support, be worn while exercising with the weights; the shoes—and socks—will give some protection. But I would heartily recommend not dropping the irons. They do not mix well with the phalanges and metatarsals. One time I almost obliterated the little toe on my right foot. *Caused by carelessness, it is my only injury in thirty-two years of weight training.*

The lifting procedures are designed to deal with the *strengths* of your body, not its weaknesses. You will lift with your legs, through the quadriceps (front thigh muscle) and through the buttocks, chest and shoulders—never the lower back—always a point of weakness.

Working with free weight, either barbells or dumbbells, you will learn how to place your body properly for each individual exercise and acquire the correct form. Most important, in the overall scheme of things, you will learn that the weight will do only what you tell it to do, both physically and mentally.

Strange as it may sound, lifts of any appreciable weight should be made mentally before they are made physically. As you stand in position, visualize that weight coming off the ground, passing your chest, and going up over your head. I promise it will go up easier. There are some weights that I could never lift physically unless I first lifted them mentally.

Though there are few lifts *but* many variations on them—presses, curls, squats, extensions, laterals, pullovers, etc.—I believe in only doing a few for all-around body conditioning. The *clean and press*—"clean" meaning to lift the barbell to shoulder level; "press" meaning to push the weight on up to full arm extension—is the ideal weight exercise for everyone, tried and true.

In the clean and press, stress and muscle action take place all the way up the body, even if the weight is only twenty pounds. There is a ripple effect. Every muscle is brought into a supporting role, from the soleus and tibia anterior at the ankles up to the muscles of the wrists and hands as the weight is fully extended.

In weight training terminology, *sets* are the types of exercises to be done during a single session. *Repetitions,* or *reps,* are the numbers of repeats of each set. So a session might have ten reps of cleans and six reps of presses; six reps of "V's"; five "flys."

My method sets a course of a few weight exercises to be accomplished in sessions lasting no longer than twenty or twenty-five minutes on a day-on, day-off basis. If you don't like Mondays, Wednesdays and Fridays, try Sunday, Tuesday and Thursday—or juggle Saturday. What must be ironclad is scheduling a *day off between lifting sessions*. The muscles that have undergone resistance need time to self-repair and rest. Sports medical specialists believe this time off is imperative. If muscles are overworked and taxed continuously, they're more apt to tear and be prone to injury.

PROGRESSIVE MUSCLE RESISTANCE

I prefer to start weight training with a new client by using an unloaded bar, the only weight being the collars, so that the lift is eighteen pounds or less, including the weight of the bar itself. There is a certain feel to the bar and a rhythm in handling it. Both must be learned.

Little by little the weight is increased. If you are already athletic and strong, the pace is quickened, and in two weeks you can be lifting ninety pounds if you weigh double that amount.

There are no absolutes in prescribing the amount of weight each person can lift. Much depends on age, sex, physical condition, body weight and time devoted to training.

For instance, a beginning female of one hundred twenty pounds, nonathletic and without prior conditioning, should lift no more than the bar and two collars the first week; two five-pound disks can be put on by the second week; change to two ten-pound disks the third week; two twenty-pound disks can be put on the fourth week.

Two sets of lifts each exercise session for the first two weeks should be expanded to three sets per session at the end of the third week. Additional sets should be added in the weeks beyond.

As the weeks pass by and disks are added to the bar, weight steadily progressing upward, your body will quickly tell you the limits. As long as the bar can be controlled, and not wave around or tilt, weight may be added to it. When you load the bar and can't lift it without great difficulty, you'll know you've reached the point of leveling off for the time being.

Breathing is as important as the weight lifting itself, particularly as the weights become heavier. As mentioned before, a properly timed breath will give you the combustion you need to handle the weight.

There are two schools of thought about breath control as applied to weight training. Both are valid; at least studies tend to support both methods. So it becomes a matter of choice. One method is to inhale *as you lift* each phase; the other method is to inhale *before* you lift, holding the air in your lungs for fuel.

The latter is my choice—taking a deep breath and holding it while I lift the weight to the *clean,* or to the shoulder position, then exhaling; inhaling deeply again, lifting the weight to the *press* position, or with arms fully extended overhead, then exhaling. I reverse the pattern for recovery. I prefer this method because I think the air held in the lungs gives support and added strength, but suggest you try both ways; use the one that works best for you.

Some instructors prescribe a series of stretches as warm-ups prior to weight training. Under almost any circumstance, stretches are fine, but I use them as interim exercises rather than warm-ups. To prepare to weight train, I take a hot shower to loosen the muscles and then go directly to the bar for warm-ups, going through the exact lifting procedure with a bare bar. After five or six repetitions, I begin slowly to add the weights.

On finishing each set, I walk away from the bar, having conquered the iron that now rests on the floor. I circle away from it and amble around for thirty or forty seconds, then do three quick and easy stretching exercises. They serve to release tension in the muscles and break up the lifting routines, fighting boredom. Then back to the irons again!

One of the marvelous things about weight training is the almost immediate visual payoff. You can watch your body shape up; watch it go through the changes. In my experience, that factor alone has had profound results. It spurs motivation.

For example, I can truthfully tell a nonathletic hundred-twenty-pound female that her body will improve if she is willing to handle three weight sessions per week, each for twenty to thirty minutes, for three months. She'll be able to see for herself in the mirror—that most severe judge of all—that her buttock sags have improved; that her shoulders and neck are firming up; and that her belly flab is disappearing.

At that point, she may ask me, "Will I have to do this the rest of my life?"

Yes, if she likes what she sees.

Those muscles have responded to progressive resistance, and they can backslide just as quickly as she can.

7

CARDIOVASCULAR ACTIVITIES: Walk, Run, Swim, Row, Ride a Bike, Jump a Rope

The wife of a famous film director called me with what she described as a "running problem." It wasn't much of one, at that. Thirtyish, she did many physical things, including racquetball and swimming. She said, "I'm into walking now. I stopped running. I walk several miles a day. Fast. I like it better than running."

I said, "Fine."

"I walk with another woman every day."

"Great," I said, refusing to argue.

What she was really trying to tell me was that for her running was boring. She needed exercise to be social. She couldn't do it alone. She'd stopped, and now she felt guilty. Nonsense!

Agreed, for most people running isn't really fun, but many of the things that are good for you somehow are not in the fun category.

Cardiovascular exercise may not be fun for all, but it is imperative if you want to be healthy, look better and live longer. Whether you walk fast, run, swim, ride a bike, jump rope or do any of the rhythmic aerobics, the circulatory system and the oxygen processing system need a workout at least three or four times a week. To really benefit the cardiovascular system, you should workout at least twenty to thirty minutes at a time.

Running, jogging, fast walking, jumping rope, riding a bike, rowing a

boat, swimming are all sustained endurance exercises. While these exercises work particular muscle groups, they all benefit the heart.

The adult fist-sized heart is the most magnificent muscle of all. Although tough and strong, it needs work to keep it strong. Exercising the heart pumps blood and its life-bearing oxygen throughout the system.

No other machine on earth is as reliable, comparably, as the human heart; none so remarkable in that the only rest it receives over a lifetime is the fraction of a second between beats. The normal heart, at rest, beats from seventy to seventy-two times per minute.

With specific cardiovascular exercise, such as running, biking and swimming, that rate can be lowered, with the actual beats stronger and deeper. The heart of an athlete can pump the same amount of blood with fifty "resting beats" when a nonathletic would require seventy similar beats for the same amount of pumped blood. On that basis, specialists have calculated that the athlete's heart beats about thirteen thousand fewer times annually than a nonathlete's.

Specific cardiovascular exercises enhance all the coronary arteries, stimulating circulation and enabling more than one blood vessel to supply a given area. Additionally, a few years back, John Holloszy, a St. Louis medical researcher, found that triglycerides, fat levels in blood, could be substantially reduced by vigorous activity. Lowering of blood fat decrease the "plaques" that clog vessels.

Over a span of years, exercises not only reduce wear and tear on the heart from lowered beating, but add directly to the general health and strength of the organ.

Running, without doubt, is the best, simplest and cheapest form of circulatory stimulant. I believe that it invigorates the cardiovascular system more than any other exercise. The total human machinery, toes to heart to blood coursing through the brain, is at work when you run. You don't have to join a club or buy any equipment to participate. Running requires no extra expenditure aside from good shoes; space is usually available somewhere, somehow, for free.

My usual rising time is dawn, more or less, and I immediately take a hot

shower to loosen muscles and awaken the skin. Next, I squeeze some fresh lemon juice into a glass of warm water and down that. Some people add a spoonful of honey.

A suggestion for those who may have problems with stomach acidity is to have a slice of whole-grain bread or a few graham crackers to help absorb the acidity so that your run will not be hindered. These kinds of foods absorb those stomach acids which build up overnight. Other runners like fresh fruit, or maybe even a few ounces of fruit juice. Nothing filling! Just enough to let your stomach know you're thinking of it. Others prefer to run on an empty stomach. Find out what works best for you and do that. Another thing I find helpful is to take along a ripe banana and have it ten or fifteen minutes after a run to help replenish the potassium in my body.

Then, after a warm-up of five stretches—Achilles, Hamstring, Tiger, Calf and Thigh, all of which I'll describe and illustrate later—I'm out on the street, pounding concrete or dirt, heeling-and-toeing with other wise ladies and gentlemen four mornings a week.

I ease into the run by slowly extending my stride, then starting the coordination of feet, legs, arms and breath, settling into an even start-up rhythm for a quarter- or half-mile; even a mile if I'm tired or sore. Then I accelerate into higher gear and maintain that rhythm.

Every human, like every car, is different, and the "driving stage" of running—the speed and distance—is an individual thing and should be one that best suits your body and endurance.

I run for about an hour in any weather, all year 'round, at an hour before the heaviest doses of smog invade the Los Angeles basin and usually reach a "runner's high." Then I'm into the shower again and off to work, charged up for the day.

While lifting weights and stretching exercises do not remotely require approval of a physician, unless there is a known medical problem, extended cardiopulmonary exercise can be chancy for some people who unknowingly have a heart condition. Safety dictates a check with your doctor prior to a program that extends beyond fast walking into jogging and running.

Specific running clothes are optional. Of course, if you want to spend money on a running wardrobe, so be it. My recommendation is high on the comfort side and low on keeping up with fashion magazines. Cold weather dictates warm, loose clothing, gloves and earmuffs; hot weather, for me, is T-shirt and nylon shorts time.

The next investment is a pair of nylon-based, name-brand shoes that fit well and are suited to the type of terrain over which you'll usually be running—concrete, asphalt, dirt paths. Ordinary street shoes or even shoes for other sports, such as basketball or tennis, won't do the job. You need both support and flexibility; and sufficient padding to absorb the uneven surfaces you'll likely encounter. Good shoes by Nike, Adidas, Puma, New Balance, Saucony or similar companies cost up to $50 or more, but are worth it. I run in Nike shoes.

Some runners prefer to run without socks, for reasons of their own, but most use either cotton or wool socks. I recommend trying socks before shifting to the naked foot. However, the decision does make a slight difference in shoe size. The shoe should always fit snug without pinching.

While I'm ambivalent about warming up to do weight lifting and actually don't think it is necessary, I'm totally for a five- or ten-minute stretch warm-up prior to the brisk walking, jogging, running, biking, rowing or similar endeavors.

Regardless of age, if you have not been engaged in some type of cardiovascular exercise of late, you should start slowly if you've selected running as the heart pumper for the months ahead. Walk briskly for half a mile four days of the first week; build up to a mile the second week. On the third week, begin a pattern of walking a block, then running a block, alternating until you've clocked approximately half a mile. After a month, extend it to two blocks walking; two running; then three, then four. After that, set your own pace. Common sense dictates that you also proceed slowly into biking or rowing, for instance. Bike for only a mile if you haven't been on one in twenty years; slowly increase the mileage as the weeks go by.

However, if the running is bringing more pain than pleasure, something is wrong. Shoes are immediately suspect, and should be checked.

Exact style and form are so individual that determining what else might be wrong is next to impossible without actual observation. I'm aware how I run: I land softly on the balls of my feet, slipping through to the toes for the next stride. It is the correct way for me. Not for everyone. It's been my experience that this method prevents lower back problems which may occur from running flat-footed.

For those who really want to know the mechanics as well as the philosophy of running, read Jim Fixx's *The Complete Book of Running*. It is one of the best books ever written on the subject, and has reached the status of "bible," for the layperson as well as for the sports specialist.

But there are those who don't like to run—people such as the director's wife—or people who don't like to walk, swim, row a boat or jump a rope. I suppose a rowing machine or stationary bike, perched in front of a TV will do, but what a waste of good scenery and fresh air!

Biking (on a real bicycle) and rowing (in a real boat) are super exercises, though not always convenient. To warm up for either, the procedure is a matter of pedaling *slowly*. Allow the muscles to loosen and the heart to get ready for a workout.

What to do in bad weather? Put on the appropriate clothing and do it anyway. It has been known to rain in Southern California and snow in Manhattan, so the less-than-hardy may opt for the indoors.

Next to running, jumping rope is an ideal all-around cardiovascular exercise, suitable for indoors, actually superior to running in the development of balance and rhythm. Definitely a bad weather exercise. A must for fighters preparing for a bout because of the balance and rhythm factors. Jumping rope

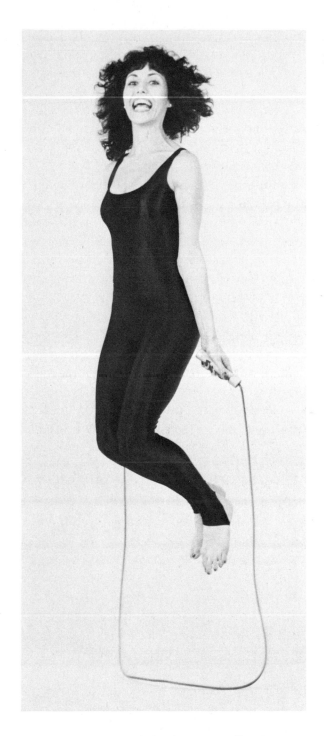

also tones up muscles in the hips, buttocks and thighs, as well as arms, shoulders and chest area.

I don't agree with those who say jumping rope is "a painful and danger-ous activity" for women because of the bouncing. I've seen wild statements about bouncing causing uterine problems, even breast cancer. A lot of women are running nowadays—"bouncing" regularly—with the blessing of their phy-sicians; 80 to 90 percent of the people enrolled in aerobics are female, and

CARDIOVASCULAR ACTIVITIES

45

aerobics are mostly bouncing, one way or another. I have yet to hear of one female who has been harmed from bouncing in either activity. I do recommend that women use proper support while running, doing aerobics, jumping rope, etc.

After childhood, the rope is put aside—because, I suspect, it is identified with childhood—and catching up again in later life is not always easy. If so, I suggest that the jumping movements be practiced without the rope, using one hand to swing the rope off to the side. In time, introduce the hand and foot coordination. Five minutes' worth of jumping rope is equal to one mile of running.

Another bad weather exercise is *squat jumps,* which are done exactly as they sound. You squat, then leap into the air, going as high as possible and returning, knees bent, to the squat position. A set of six to eight should be accomplished. The old *jumping jacks* of childhood or running in place are also alternatives in rainy or frigid weather.

Water exercise is excellent for people with back problems or degenerative changes in the body joints. Swimming is an especially good cardiovascular exercise for "problem cases" because the body is supported by the water, and stress on individual parts of the body can be either avoided or reduced.

The key to good physical and mental health is to stimulate the entire cardiovascular system—in any way you prefer. Without that system in good shape, lifting weights and stretching is of little use anyway.

FOOD AWARENESS:
Whatever You Eat, Make Sure That Plenty of It Is Fresh, Green and Fiber Filled

New clients often ask, "What should I do about my diet? There are so many diets on the market. Which one is best?"

Do they buy Pritikin, Atkins, Stillman, Bieler, Scarsdale or Weight Watchers?

Well, I certainly wouldn't recommend the high-protein, low-carbohydrate Stillman or Atkins programs. The partaker might not have the strength to lift a weight, stretch a triceps or run two miles.

My answer is, usually, "I'll tell you, in a general way, what has worked best for me for more than twenty years."

Simply because of the never-ending stream of diets, I cringe from the word and use the term food awareness instead, which is really what it is all about. In fact, I refuse to recommend any diet concept because so many of them are in conflict. There is no unanimous verdict on any single food plan from nutritionists, doctors or the federal government. While individual doctors have endorsed one diet or another, argument continues over high- and low-carbohydrate diets; high- and low-protein diets; high- and low-cholesterol diets; vitamins, minerals; you name it.

What most people seldom think of is nature's direct, sometimes mischievous role in body structure—inherited physical characteristics of parents. The genes, for better or worse, have been passed along and the battle, quite often, is against the "bad" genes. It is then a "mind over matter" fight, with the mind directing the body to take corrective action—proper eating habits and effective exercise.

Clothing often collaborates with the bad genes—on purpose or not—hiding the fat deposits in strategic places. I don't really blame anyone for secreting fat temporarily, but permanently hiding it under coats and flowing dresses is to play a fool's game. Beneath the folds of cloth, the fat increases.

Some people look at a model with an eighteen-inch waist and think, She must workout like crazy to get that waistline. Not necessarily so! In many cases, because of genes, she has inherited the small waist.

Genes aside, almost everyone has specific areas of the body that tend to take on fat deposits. The general areas usually first affected are the abdomen, buttocks, hips and thighs, comparatively easy targets for harboring fat.

The first step to ridding the body of fat deposits is mental rather than physical—the determination to tackle the problem. I think the driving force should be very simple, straightforward and entirely selfish: will I look and feel better after I lose all this fat? The answer is within ourselves.

At the point of determination, most people, I've found, begin to look for "gimmicks" that will slice off the fat painlessly and without too much effort: a certain diet, or a certain diet-plus-exercise plan. As aforementioned, there are plenty of diets and plans to choose from, but *the key is mental*—the will to do it—not the program, mine or any other.

I have certain rigid general rules that I apply to the waging of war against fat deposits: 1. No crash dieting. Areas that aren't a home for fat will surely suffer, sometimes causing a "gaunt look." 2. Be patient. It took a while to build up the fat. Give yourself an appropriate time to undo the damage. 3. Beware of the bargaining or barter system. ("I can have this cake today if I fast tomorrow.") Yes, you can, but todays and tomorrows often get mixed up. Bargain with yourself infrequently. 4. Stay away from the scales! Don't play the numbers game. If the numbers don't fall quickly, people trying to develop food awareness often become discouraged. The mirror and the fit of your clothes are better barometers.

During the mid-1950s, when few people paid much attention to what went into their stomachs, and there were no best-selling diet books around, I began to chart a middle-of-the road, commonsense course that now coincides with parts and pieces of Dr. Henry Bieler's *Food Is Your Best Medicine* and Nathan Pritikin's *The Pritikin Program for Diet and Exercise*. Again, common sense is the key. I don't recall ever looking at a diet book until the mid-1960s.

Many children, perhaps even most, are told that sweets are bad for them, principally because of tooth decay, brown sugar included. There is *no good refined sugar,* brown or white, no matter its origin, cane or beets.

I quit sweets when I was about sixteen, not because a dentist, doctor or nutritionist told me to, but because I was a gym buff and thought that cake and candy might make me fat. Good reasoning, I now realize.

I started on a fresh-fruit kick as a teenager in Florida simply because it was on the table, hardly realizing that my body was receiving plenty of natural sugar and had no need for refined sugar. The reason I ate fruit was because it tasted good.

A menu heavy on vegetables, chicken and fish, and light on beef and pork began in the Broadway days because the former was cheaper. As time went by, the daily intake became predominately fresh vegetables and leafy greens.

I'd guess that if you are health oriented because of parental advice or role-modeling, good eating habits will more or less continue throughout a lifetime. I'd also estimate that few Americans born in the 1930s, 1940s and even the '50s had such advice and role modeling. Unfortunately, we're an overweight nation riddled with bad eating habits. Diet book best-sellers are a partial proof; heart attack victims are another.

Aside from common sense—I didn't need a doctor or nutritionist to guess that fresh vegetables are superior in every way to canned ones—I had no sophistication about food until the 1960s when I began working with the high-energy people of the Broadway stage.

They talked in terms of calories and proteins and carbohydrates and enzymes and calcium. They ate kale and collards and mustard greens to vary their diet from spinach and broccoli and Brussels sprouts. They ate raw spinach rather than the cooked variety. *They thought about what they ate.* They said, "For God's sake, don't eat sugar or salt." (Not for *His* sake, but your own.)

They said, "eat high-fiber" foods although I was unknowingly already well into that. For years high-fiber foods had been recommended for older people to help with bowel elimination. "Hey, wow, they're for everyone!"

What all this did for me was to make me stop, for the first time in my life, and really think about what was going into my body. I was solely responsible for that choice. What an awakening!

Between rehearsals and workouts and shows, Broadway dancers burn up more energy than ditchdiggers. They require the correct fuel to sustain their activities. Furthermore, their livelihood depends on how they look and how they perform. I doubt that there is a greater incentive.

Perhaps I am oversimplifying it, but for me the most important thing about food and diet is a matter of what you eat versus what you burn up. What you don't burn up is potential trouble. Fat is the unwanted and dangerous residue.

In formulating a physical fitness and body sculpting program, I've found that no single approach works because each person is usually different in terms of physical condition, habits, temperament, work routines, needs and desires.

The same applies to food awareness. Some people want to lose weight radically; others just a few pounds. Still others want to maintain the weight they have.

"Will I lose weight by running?" Very likely.

"Will I lose weight by lifting weights?" Not very likely—but you will firm, tone and strengthen your body.

The woman who is raising small children, doing housekeeping and cooking, has to have a different schedule than the computer saleswoman. She also burns up much more energy daily than the saleswoman. Her time will be different; her diet somewhat different. Her nearness to the refrigerator is also a possible hazard.

The male who commutes a hundred twenty miles a day, round-trip, to his office has a different dietary and exercise problem than the telephone lineman who goes to work at 7:00 A.M. and is off at 4:00.

Almost fifty nutrients are needed to maintain wellness and fitness in the human body. All of them can be found within what the daily intake of carbohydrates, protein, minerals, fat, vitamins and water should be. None are special; all are easily available.

I have problems with super diets and special food supplements. I'm often asked, "Should I take desiccated liver?" My answer is, "If you want to, but how about some fresh broccoli?"

HOW MANY CALORIES A DAY?

This book is about physical fitness and exercising, not about food and diet, yet one must go with the other. Food is fuel and energy. But how many calories?

The one absolute in losing weight is you must take in fewer calories than you burn. You must select foods which contain fewer calories and increase your activities.

Fact—a pound of body fat contains 3,500 calories. If a person needs to lose one pound of fat, that person needs to burn up 3,500 calories more than he or she consumes. Let's say a person is taking in 3,500 calories a day and wants to lose two pounds a week (I consider this to be a safe weight loss), that person should cut their calorie intake by 1,000 calories a day.

Only by slowly and conscientiously accelerating our calorie loss over a set period of time can we avoid the effects of nutritional deficiencies, menstrual irregularities, infertility, hair loss, skin changes, cold intolerances, constipation and even psychiatric changes. Don't always be too strict with yourself because it is a human trait to be self-indulgent. What I usually suggest is to measure your calorie intake carefully for four or five days, then add a treat on the sixth or seventh day.

Most importantly, remember that thin is not necessarily fit. Use common sense in determining your weight and remember that body structure, exercise, jobs, climate and many other factors can alter or affect your weight.

ABOUT FATS

THE CACCIOTTI METHOD

Fats are with us to stay. Fat in the body acts as insulation, padding for internal organs, lubrication and as a storehouse when activity has robbed muscle of glycogen, the muscle sugar (fuel). So there's a place for fat, which comes in two categories: saturated and unsaturated. The former is found in animals and most specialists believe that it is the dangerous one, an invitation to eventual heart trouble. Unsaturated fats are found in plants, and are less likely to cause circulatory difficulties.

The problem, of course, lies with the intake of fats, both vegetable and animal. Some fat is necessary for digestive purposes but the average person consumes 50 percent more than needed. Less than four ounces of sirloin steak has 77 percent fat; ham, in the same amount, is also in the seventies; bologna is three-quarters fat. A hamburger is one-third fat, so the McDonald's / Burger King / Wendy's "fast food generation" may be in for a lot of trouble. But even a ripe olive is one-quarter fat.

So eat sparingly—if at all—of meats, dairy products, egg yolks, nuts, avocado; shun cooking oils and lard. Oils are 100 percent fat. Margerine is bad, but butter is worse. For my potato, I opt for the lesser of two evils— avocado, mashed and spread across the top, with fresh papaya chunks. Delicious—but not too often.

Food awareness *is* painful.

Cholesterol is a fat-like substance that is a normal part of blood and all body tissue. It is essential for the synthesis of certain important hormones. There are several different forms of blood cholesterol. When too much is present in your bloodstream, it can contribute to the clogging of your arteries and increase your risk of heart attack. Some cholesterol is supplied by the food you eat, but your own liver produces it even if you have *no* cholesterol in your diet.

Science is divided about the connection between the fats and cholesterol we eat, the cholesterol and triglycerides in our blood, and heart disease. While the debate over proof rages on, U.S. officials advise that we cut down on all fat intake.

Choose lean meat, fish, poultry, dry beans and peas as your protein sources—make moderate use of eggs and organ meats (such as liver). Limit intake of butter, cream, hydrogenated margerines, shortenings and coconut oil, as well as foods made from these products. Trim excess fat off meats and poultry. Broil, bake or boil rather than fry. Read labels carefully to determine both amount and type of fat contained in foods. Unless your doctor advises you that your cholesterol levels are too high, don't feel that you must totally avoid high cholesterol foods such as shellfish, organ meats and eggs. They can be plentiful sources of the protein and important vitamins and minerals you need. *Moderate.* Don't eliminate.

Look at yourself, everything that's noticeable—eyes, hair, skin, nails— is essentially protein. Your muscles, including those that are moving your eyes as you read this are made up of protein tissues.

I think, and hope, that the day of the high-protein diet is gone. While it is true that the body needs some protein to regenerate itself, and also true that a high-protein diet was quite popular in the past, medical researchers discovered that the liver and kidneys had to work overtime to process the barrage of proteins. A recurring complaint of high-protein dieters was constipation, resulting in irritability and fatigue. There is far more bulk in a basic carbohydrate intake, which aids bowel movement.

In the protein column are meats, nuts, olives, cheese, dairy products, eggs (yolks), fish, fowl, peanuts, soybeans and some seeds, such as sunflower and pumpkin. Avocado again, alas. Learn to balance and manage your intake of protein. Chicken and fish have less fat and are healthier than beef or pork. Also, you'll find yourself eating less chicken or fish than, perhaps, nuts, olives or cheeses.

ABOUT CARBOHYDRATES

Thankfully, the day of "carbs," the starches—in companionship with fresh vegetables—has arrived. Natural, or *complex,* carbohydrates that dwell in whole grains, rice, potatoes, legumes and other vegetables and fruits, *create pure energy* without all the drawbacks of high proteins and fats. The carbs do contain protein, but are not high in calories. The caloric problems arise when they are doused with rich sauces, gravies, butter, oils and cheeses. I think the starches have come back to stay (not that they ever went far away) and they include, happily, whole-wheat pasta. Insofar as my conditioning program is concerned, eat plentifully of carbohydrates.

Fat "burns" slowly in the body, but the carbs burn quickly. Protein is another "bad burner," taking a lot of oxygen. The carbs are easy on oxygen, easy on excretion.

Super runner Bill Rogers eats high-carb foods for several days before a marathon to store up glycogens, the principal carbohydrate energy material. Many other athletes take the same route before big events.

In comparatively rare cases, there is carbohydrate intolerance. The best and easiest way to overcome the system's rebellion is to introduce carbs into the diet in very small amounts—a tablespoonful of milled whole grain three times a day; after a month increase it to two tablespoons three times a day. An aid to digestion of carbohydrates is the enzyme Pan-5.

ABOUT FIBER

We all talk about pollution and the environment. What we must also consider is what helps regulate our internal environment—the environment of our cells and tissues that affect our health and well being. Fiber is what acts as our internal regulator.

Most people associate fiber with laxatives, and while this is true, fiber can also maintain the proper bulk weight which is required for proper digestion that eventually aids in controlling diarrhea. Fiber also contains properties which bind with calcium, magnesium and other minerals before they are absorbed in your body.

Fibers are found in a variety of foods which come from three natural sources—grains, fruits and vegetables. The combination of these fibers in your daily diet all help in promoting a healthy and clean "inner you." Don't "overkill" with one type of fiber, but balance your foods so that all three are part of your diet.

More and more information is being discovered about the minerals that animals—including humans—get from the earth via plant life. What we definitely know is that minerals are absolutely essential to all bodily functions. Potassium, calcium, copper, iron and magnesium are important minerals for the different parts of your body such as your bones, muscles, heart, eyes, skin, gums and teeth; zinc is very good for your eyes as well as for your reproductive organs, and sodium helps your skin, gums, teeth and eyes.

You may have experienced fatigue during or after a workout because you're missing two important minerals—potassium and magnesium. As I previously mentioned, I usually eat a ripe banana to take care of my potassium deficiency, and I take wheat germ or seeds and nuts to replenish the magnesium lacking in my system.

Mineral supplements prescribed by a physician or nutritionist can help, but I'm a firm believer in choosing a wide variety of fruits and vegetables, which would be a natural, sound and beneficial way of furnishing your mineral needs.

ABOUT MINERALS

Most of the natural grain cereals are sold in the major supermarkets and health food stores. On my shelf are Crawford's Toasted Bran, Erewhon No. 9 Granola with Bran, 100% Natural Bran Cereal. Use any of the whole, barely refined grains that strike your fancy and taste: cracked wheat, oats (the old-fashioned slow-cooking kind)—topped with a tablespoon of both wheat germ and unrefined bran (not the manufactured, sweetened kind).

Buckwheat cakes cooked in a Teflon or similar-type pan and livened up with a fresh fruit topping are a change of pace for breakfast.

For breads, use the whole-grain variety. White bread from highly refined flour is a depth charge in your stomach. Whole-wheat pita bread is my favorite, lunch or dinner.

GRAINS FOR BREAKFAST AND THEREAFTER

Water, water, pure and pristine—if you can get it. I recommend six to eight glasses daily, but never with meals. A glass half an hour before meals and half an hour—more or less—after meals takes care of your water needs to perfection. Water with meals washes out other nutrients and interferes with the digestive process.

Water is like breathing: we pay little attention to it until we really need it. Yet water is the one liquid necessary to almost every body function: blood circulation, urination, cell building. Dehydration can put a stop to body efficiency and eventually cause death. Some people worry about becoming internally waterlogged. Providing you have normal kidney function, that is the least of your worries, and even a gallon a day won't hurt you. In hot weather, the more the better.

SOMETHING TO DRINK

FOOD AWARENESS

53

The reason I prefer bottled water to what comes out of the tap is a matter of asbestos, among other little floaters. Tests of tap water in major population centers indicate a level of asbestos too high for my long-term comfort. Although the jury is still out on its cancer-causing properties, medical science does know that asbestos damages mucous membranes.

Fresh fruit juices, if you can afford them, are highly recommended, though some people have acidity problems; use bottled, without additives, if you can't afford the fresh.

Milk? Use nonfat or acidophilus low-fat milk if you must. However, no adult needs milk of any variety, and most physicians, despite the milk lobby, will say that milk isn't really needed after age twelve; even that age is arbitrary.

Coffee? No. Use decaffeinated if you must, but sparingly. Postum, made from bran, wheat and molasses and which doesn't contain any caffeine, gets my vote. No sugar.

Tea? Yes, if you use herbal teas—rosehips, mint, lemon, mandarin orange, papaya, to name a few. No sugar and limit use of milk, honey and artificial sweeteners.

No soda pop, diet or not.

ALCOHOL HOUR

The evening institution of predinner alcohol mainly benefits distilleries, booze distributors and the tax collectors. The chemical certainly doesn't benefit the human body, even heart patients. Blood, heart, liver and brain are all under attack when subjected to a single ounce of alcohol. Use liquor, wine, beer and ale sparingly, if at all.

A good cocktail hour substitute is club soda with a lemon twist.

An occasional glass of wine before dinner shouldn't upset any crusader for health and fitness. Two glasses for birthdays, holidays, parties. After all, I'm Italian.

THE DINNER BELL

Many experts quarrel over when to ring the dinner bell. Some experts say to eat when you're hungry, 3:00 A.M., or 3:00 P.M. That's well and good for those who don't have a blessed thing to do all day and night. But meal-hour habits aren't to be broken easily, and practicality will win.

Long ago dinner was served at the midday hour and supper was a lighter meal served at dusk, minus daylight saving. Though we'll never return to that healthy pattern, the folks of yore had the right idea. The body just doesn't like to be stuffed two hours before bedtime. Flat-on-the-back-digestion is the hard way. Ideally, the heaviest meal should come in the middle of the day, but that is impossible for most people and would slow the afternoon work. But the evening meal, now the heaviest, should be consumed as far prior to bedtime as possible. Dinner at eight, though fashionable, is intestinal first-degree murder, and leaves calories unburned.

Whatever is wrong with the world, it isn't fresh vegetables! They are loaded with carbs, and low on calories. Raw vegetables are the best because cooking reduces their nutritional value. But since sameness is dullness, I suggest you vary the types and combinations of vegetables you eat. Lightly steam or bake—avoid over-cooking, frying or drowning them in butter, oils, sauces and salt. I use lemon, lime and parsley flakes as seasoning. Also, some people may find steamed vegetables easier to digest than raw ones.

From *A* to *Z*—artichokes, which are high in calories, to zucchini, which is comparatively low—you have more than fifty to choose from, many of which are on the stands all year 'round. Eat what you prefer. Eat until hunger is gone.

I pay special attention to the salad group—the lettuces (particularly romaine and spinach, for the dark color indicates more nutrients), Spanish and green and red onions, bean sprouts, mushrooms, carrots, zucchini, celery. For midmorning or midafternoon snacks: carrots, celery, zucchini, cauliflower buds.

Potatoes—new and old, white rose or red, sweet and yams—are great fuel. They provide potassium, phosphorus and iron as well. I eat potatoes two or three times a week, but never fried. French fries and home fries are small fat bombs.

The versatile legume or bean family—green or snap, kidney, lima, navy, pinto, garbanzo, black, peas and others—offer fine main dishes or soups. I have a bean dish, in some form, twice a week.

In the vegetable soup department, my *Joy of Cooking* lists forty-five possibilities.

Depending on the season, and the region in which you live, frozen vegetables are sometimes cheaper than fresh, although they aren't as tasty or nutritious.

Though some nutritionists either approve or do not object to canned vegetables and soups—or the dried or powdered versions of both—I'm opposed to them because of the additives and the salt and sugar content. At the same time, I realize that many people must eat canned food because they can't afford to do otherwise. If it is necessary to consume canned goods of any type, including fruit juices—read the labels and select the most natural kinds.

High in carb content, most fruits have negligible fat content. Only dates, figs and raisins, among the common fruits, while low in fat, are caloric disasters. Fresh fruit has 100 percent approval on my list, and I'd recommend it for breakfast, lunch and dinner as a supplement.

Citrus fruit is in a category by itself in providing ascorbic acid—Vitamin C—to the body. I'd recommend it once daily, fresh squeezed or whole. I have a fruit salad, sometimes with unsalted nuts, twice a week.

CANNED VEGETABLES AND SOUPS

THE FRUIT DEPARTMENT

FOOD AWARENESS

FISH AND FOWL   Fish or chicken, alternating every other day, portions not to exceed six to eight ounces, maintains a balanced diet. Both fish and fowl should be skinned, then boiled, broiled or baked—never fried. I serve mine with lemon juice and fresh, fine, chopped parsley.

BEEF AND PORK AND LAMB   I am strongly against all red meat cooked and served in any fashion, but if you must, please order the leanest cuts, and even then slice away any visible fat. Items made with by-products, such as sausages and frankfurters, are usually laced with additives and are totally disastrous. Protein from beef, pork and lamb is a real Trojan horse dietetically, despite what the red meat lobby says. In 1974, the Food and Nutrition Board of the National Academy of Sciences said that meat is not essential to health.

DAIRY PRODUCTS   Milk commercials aside, I recommend you avoid whole milk and cream. When it's a must, use nonfat milk or acidophilus low-fat milk. Cheddar, Swiss, Roquefort and other members of that family are all high-calorie and high-fat. Butter is the calorie heavyweight of all bovine products. However, cottage cheese, the dieter's staple, is fine to use but only if it's low-fat—no more than 4%. Natural low-fat yogurt, without added sugar or fruit preserves, is also a winner.

EGGS   If the yolk of an egg behaved nutritionally the way the white does, I'd be for the hens of the world. Unfortunately, raw yolks have 59 calories and a cholesterol count of 312 compared with the raw egg white which has a calorie count of 17 and a cholesterol count of zero. If the egg habit cannot be broken, have them poached—no more than three times a week.

COOKING OILS: SATURATED, UNSATURATED   Oils are awful for you. Vegetable or animal. What's a person to do? Bake, broil or use a Teflon-type pan. Just a look at pure lard will tell you that the best purpose for it would be to grease machinery, not the human body.

MAYONNAISE   Mayonnaise is the great American sandwich spreader and salad mixer, but it happens to be another diet hazard with 109 calories per tablespoon, plus its fat residue. While there are substitutes for mayonnaise, such as mock sour cream made from nonfat buttermilk and cottage cheese, I prefer the nonsugar, nonfat, nonsalt types available at health food stores.

What is most important in food awareness is that you have the power— mental and physical—to shape your body the way you want it.

THE CACCIOTTI METHOD   When your body does satisfy you, "fire it," as the potter does when placing his form into the kiln, locking the condition of fitness, polishing it from time to time.

56

9

ABOUT VITAMINS

If everyone ate the proper foods, in exactly the proper amounts, there'd be no need for manufactured vitamins. That very profitable industry would close down overnight. Fact is, nature has provided the necessary vitamins and minerals in a wide variety of vegetables and fruits, but taste, time and trouble seem to prevent us from taking advantage of this health storehouse.

Yellow in fruits and vegetables indicates that vitamin A is present and bountiful. Yellow squash is an A storehouse, for instance. Raw broccoli is rich in A and C; raw cabbage is rich in C. I could go on for pages, courtesy of the U.S. Department of Agriculture, but few of us will ever eat the right combinations daily to provide health needs.

Except for vitamin C, I'm against mega-doses of any vitamin or mineral. I'm also against manufactured vitamins that use synthetic bases rather than natural ones.

I'm a moderate yet consistant vitamin taker of A, B, C, D, E and extra pantothenic acid (member of the vitamin B family) along with the mineral supplement, calcium-magnesium. I also take two capsules of acidophilus with pectin directly after eating. For me, this aids the digestive process considerably.

Vitamin A helps in maintaining healthy skin as well as in fighting infection, increasingly important in areas with high levels of air pollution, where people are more susceptible to infection and colds, such as in New York and Los Angeles. Vitamin A is also important for the maintenance of good eyesight, especially night vision. Vitamin D should be taken in combination with A, in the same capsule. D promotes growth of bones and teeth. I take 5,000 IU of A and 400 IU of D daily.

High B complex is an essential part of my daily vitamin program. B vitamins help provide the body with energy by converting nutrients into energy and body tissue; they assist the metabolic process and fight fatigue. B complex is a must for people in high-pressure occupations. I take one 125-milligram (time released) tablet daily.

Pantothenic acid, part of the B complex, improves the body's ability to withstand stress and fatigue. In addition, it helps to prevent premature aging and wrinkles. It is thought to be essential for cell growth and helpful in preventing gray hair. I take two daily, 250 milligrams each.

Vitamin C, also known as ascorbic acid, is frequently used in the prevention and treatment of the common cold. The use of vitamin C to combat cancer is now a remarkable possibility. Along with vitamin A, it appears to maintain healthy gums and increases resistance to infection and promotes the healing of wounds. C seems to be especially effective if taken in combination with bioflavonoids, found in the white lining of grapefruit, essential to the absorption of vitamin C and also helpful in building protection against infections. Your body's need for vitamin C increases when under conditions of stress, smoking and air pollution. Since high levels of C cannot be maintained in the body, it is best taken in reasonable doses throughout the day. I take at least 1,000 milligrams daily, more when fighting a cold. People with acidity problems might find granulated C, diluted in fluids, easier to handle.

Vitamin E is another pollution fighter. It acts as an antioxidant in the body, preventing the breakdown and toxic recombination of certain substances. E is considered by many cardiologists to be a major weapon in the treatment and prevention of heart disease. I take 1,000 units daily.

In addition to these vitamins, I take calcium-magnesium daily. Imperative for the maintenance of strong, healthy bones and teeth, this mineral combination also helps the nervous system (alleviating stress, insomnia and depression). By assisting in blood clotting and in the expansion and contraction of muscles and heart rhythm, these minerals help prevent heart attacks. Studies have shown that people, especially women, show an increased need for these minerals as the aging process progresses. Women after the age of menopause are highly susceptible to osteoporosis, or bone softening. This situation can and has been corrected by daily doses of calcium and magnesium.

Calcium-magnesium also works to ease other common symptoms associated with aging and is often prescribed to relieve premenstrual, menstrual or menopause discomfort. Calcium-magnesium comes in tablets in a 2 to 1 ratio—twice as much calcium as magnesium. Dolomite is a natural form of the two minerals obtained from dolomite mines. I prefer the new chelated form derived from natural sources. I take a minimum of 400 milligrams calcium, 200 milligrams magnesium—3 chelated tablets per day.

Along with the above vitamins, a daily must for me is acidophilus, a natural culture which reestablishes and reenforces beneficial bacterial flora in the intestinal tract. Along with being a good digestive aid, it is also used for problems such as stomach ulcers, diverticulosis, colitis and yeast infections.

In recent years, thankfully, the medical profession has become less resistant to nutrition and vitamin use. If you consult a doctor or nutritionist, be sure it's one who can properly guide you in establishing your daily vitamin and mineral program.

10

MOTIVATION:
Stripping in Front of a Mirror
Is the Best Motivation of All

I'm as weak as the next person when it comes to pasta, ice cream and chocolate mousse.

I don't like to watch my diet.

I don't like to lift weights.

I don't like to stretch.

I don't like to run.

I hate getting up at 5:30 A.M. after four hours of sleep, especially in the winter. Even the dog is yawning.

I hate all these things, but I love the response I receive from my body when I do. I love the feeling and I love what I see in the mirror. My body thanks me every day.

Tomorrow I've got to get up at six and lift heavy weights.

I can't stand the thought of going into that gym, but I know I must go. And I know that I can't just go in and pick up that barbell in front of the mirror and have negative thoughts. That bar has 250 pounds of weight on it and it won't go over my head unless I am mentally and physically ready at 6:30 A.M. I'll have to be sucking and puffing all that oxygen to get my energy up and my blood flowing.

I'm saying good morning to my body. "In a little while, you'll have to bust buns. Not cheerfully, nor willingly, but, buddy, you've got to do it. You're all I have or ever will have."

Oddly enough, the body is hoping you will work it. It wants to be utilized; wants to be walked and run and stretched; wants to be robust and healthy.

Early in the morning, of course, is the roughest time to do anything but sleep. You have all the excuses. The bed is warm and soft. You can think about having a good breakfast. You can even sell yourself on staying in bed.

"I can miss today. I, Tony Cacciotti, can afford to miss today because I'm in pretty good shape." But I *can't* really afford it for the simple reason that my body will miss it. Each time I work out, my body talks to me. *"Hey, thanks, you're still with me!"*

Working out is not something you like to do but something you have to do. I don't really know anyone who works with weights who really likes them. I've run with hundreds of people, including many professional athletes, and I don't know one who'd rather pound his/her heels than stay in bed or drink a beer or watch the morning TV shows.

You do it because you must do it.

A man I'll call Frank did it because he had to do it to survive. He had Parkinson's disease, that incurable degenerative brain malfunction that comes on in mid-to-late life, causing body tremors and muscular rigidity.

Frank was fifty-five years old, with wealth, position, everything money could buy, but he was in deep physical trouble. When I met him, he was trying to work out in a Manhattan gym—a feeble, embarrassing, act of desperation to him. Yet I was impressed with his courage all the more.

He could not control his steps and would often lunge forward, losing his balance. If he did stay erect, he would shake pitifully. The shaking would continue after he sat down to rest. Just watching him was painful.

His speech was jerky, and his head bobbed while he said, "I don't think you can do anything with me, but I'm a very positive person and I'll pay you well."

Frank became my first medical client back in 1962 and he was indeed a very positive person. I knew nothing about Parkinson's, but I was willing to attempt to rejuvenate his muscles; attempt to strengthen him so that he could stop or reduce the lunging. Building support muscles was a primary goal.

Before the first session, I said, "I'm going to treat you the same way I treat everyone else. I'm not going to change any of the exercises." He was pleased and nodded that he approved.

I had a hunch that the resistance of weights would help those atrophying muscles. I believed that the yoga and dance exercises, in combination with the barbells and dumbbells, would be an initial step toward decreasing the shakes, loosening the body and increasing his balance.

Looking forward to each session, exhilarated by the slim signs of any improvement, I worked with him three days a week at a private gym in New York or was flown to Florida to work with him down there. Each session was supposedly to be only an hour, but I don't remember many that didn't last two hours.

"Lift that foot, Frank. Hold it! Put it down, now lift it again! Now the other one. C'mon, Frank. You can do it.

"Go up on your toes now and stretch that arm. Stretch it. Stretch it, dammit. Reach for the ceiling, Frank. Reach for it. See yourself going up, see yourself reaching."

I wanted him to realize which muscles were at work; which ones were going to help in the fight against the palsy. The second week in the gym I had him doing presses with eighteen pounds of weight. The bar shook and wobbled over his head but stayed up there.

Two months later tears were brimming in my eyes as I watched him clean and press forty pounds.

Frank will never be cured of Parkinson's, but the man I saw in New York in 1964, after our final session, had new mobility; any lunging that he did was controlled; the tremors had lessened. He could wage both a physical and mental battle against his illness.

He'd motivated himself. I was simply the supportive, teaching and reminding voice.

I saw him eight years later and, remarkably, as he aged he'd held the ground he'd gained, despite the constant inroads of the disease.

A lady in California, a cancer patient I'll call Joan, also comes to mind. Her sister-in-law, who was one of the most positive-thinking persons I'd ever met, brought her to me. Joan, about fifty years old, had lost all of her hair, had lost a lot of weight, and was understandably depressed. The cancer was in remission, but the woman couldn't bring herself even to look at her own body. She'd once been a very pretty woman with a good figure.

As with Frank, I really made no concessions. Instead, I set goals and asked how hard she was willing to work to restore her body.

At first there was resentment, barely hidden anger at the ravages of cancer, a sulkiness and skepticism. "Either you want to keep that body you have now or you want to do something about it," I told her.

In the weeks that followed, I caught Joan glancing at herself in the mirror, watching as the leotard began to fill out and as radiance came back into her skin.

A teacher can only demonstrate and advise. The motivation that counts comes from within. *She wanted to change!*

The third example of motivation was a thirty-five-year-old British business executive. In 1979, I went to London as a consultant to Cavendish Leisure, Ltd., a consortium of five English companies and one American firm, Carter Hawley Hale. Cavendish was exploring ways of developing enterprises in the leisure field, but I went over specifically to advise on the reduction of stress through health and fitness.

Four males, ages ranging from thirty-five to seventy, were to be my fitness-stress guinea pigs for a period of two weeks during which daily gym sessions would be held, pointing toward a pilot program to help reduce stress through exercise.

One candidate—I'll call him Oscar—was of particular interest. The man who had hired me, Sir Anthony Burney, chairman of Debenhams, Ltd., a consortium member, told me, "Oscar is an extremely bright, highly paid executive who is very dissatisfied with his physical appearance."

Though I was supposed to be concentrating on a program that would reduce stress, I was intrigued by this man who was obviously ashamed of what his skin encased.

Actually, Oscar wasn't enormous. He was just flabby, round-shouldered and uncoordinated. Not a monster, but self-conscious and anguished. I had lunch with him and watched him gobble rich food and down a bottle of wine.

The reason for his weight and poor posture was a total lack of physical exercise. He didn't so much as walk around the block. Though he didn't seem to realize it, his main problem was that he was a candidate for a fatal heart attack. His appearance in the company of trim junior executives was a secondary problem.

I soon realized that the chances of Oscar going on the meaningful diet were remote. The man couldn't resist food. The solution then was to replace the flab with muscle tone by using weights, to put him on a vigorous cardio-vascular program and work on his balance and body control. He needed to take away the waddle and replace it with the walk and attitude of a fit, confident male. Most importantly, he had to adjust his thinking: heavy men could appear trim, too.

Oscar did all this over a year's time and now operates with confidence and ease. He weighs about what he did before, but what is on his body now is muscle and not fat.

Though prodded by me and others, the motivation to do it came from within.

Admittedly, these are extreme examples of people with grave or poten-tially grave physical problems, but I think each illustrates that a radical life situation can be turned around by willpower and determination.

No physical fitness program can be of value without the person making the decision to become fit and then making a commitment to carry it out. Although there are training shortcuts, there is no easy, absolutely painless way to take the body from a state of long abuse to one of fitness.

Yet no other endeavor is likely to bring as much support from family and friends. As the shape-up of your body becomes apparent, you'll hear the rooting from the sidelines. Having a friend pat your belly and tell you that you're bulging is a terrible kick in the ego. Having a friend say, "Gee, you look super" spurs you on, in addition to sending the ego skyward.

In the reverse, I've had clients who want to be continually back-slapped; constantly told they're doing well. They say, "Please tell me I'm looking better," after ten days of hard work. I say, frankly, "No, you're not. Look in the mirror."

MOTIVATION

In this day of instant gratification, they don't want to hear that. They hate me for it, knowing it is true. Two days later, they'll call, "Tony, I'm sorry. I really want you to be honest."

Being honest is saying that results can be seen and felt by the end ot a month if the client is willing to work out a minimum of six days a week, five and a half hours out of the one hundred sixty-eight available.

I repeat that I firmly believe the best motivator of all is the full-length mirror. It never tells a lie. It is ruthless, as it should be.

Aside from the pages of this book, there is no way for me to personally motivate you toward fitness and a better body.

Why not try the mirror test? Strip down, stand before it. Turn one way, then the other.

Do you like what you see?

If not, take this book to heart, head and muscle, and go for total fitness!

The Exercises

ABOUT THE EXERCISES YOU'LL SOON DO

Though the purposes overlap, I divide exercises into three categories: those for *flexibility,* those for *strength* and those for *stamina.* All three categories are needed in the building and maintenance of the body, in the maintenance of wellness.

Genetics and other factors play major roles in the structure of the human form, but we also have the unique opportunity, as owners of the body, to be architects and builders of flexibility, strength and stamina.

In working with clients, I begin with *balance and control,* testing for balance not so much for what I learn, but to make the average client completely—and shockingly—aware of an inability to perform the simple function of keeping equilibrium while rising on the toes. That jolt of awareness is usually the key to everything else that follows. The balance and control exercises are the foundation of the entire building program, especially flexibility.

The *stretching* exercises, next in line, are designed to do a multiplicity of things: aid in balance and control, isolate certain muscles for certain toning—bust, leg, thigh, neck, etc.; promote flexibility, strength and stamina. In my opinion, stretches are *the* uni-purpose, uni-sex, uni-age, uni-wonderful exercises of the whole workout world. As we grow older, our body's need for them increases.

Lifting is purely and simply for strength, with the added bonus of enhancing your looks. With weights, you can isolate and emphasize specific muscles in all parts of the body. A special gift from weight training is the development or deepening of confidence.

THE EXERCISES

66

The *cardiovascular* group may well be the most important of all. Without a strong heart and good circulatory system, your fine muscles might as well be hollow. Whether it is running, jogging, fast walking, biking, swimming, rowing or jumping rope, the cardiovascular activities are the life sustainers and must be given that recognition.

Any of these exercises can be done singularly or with partners or in groups. Two can row a boat as well as one, maybe better; most sidewalks are wide enough for dual running or fast walking; a swimming partner is always a good idea, though conversation is limited. Even three can be involved in jumping rope, as I remember form the "red hot pepper" days of youth.

As I hope I've indicated, I make no special allowance for pre-senior citizens or senior citizens. I think it is an insult to assume people approaching or over sixty can't perform every exercise or routine in this book. Photographs of the models indicate age has no limits here.

Though I realize that there are limitations, that the old-school "label" distinctions must be made—*beginner, intermediate* and *advanced,* insofar as certain exercises are concerned—my general rule is to let the exerciser listen to his or her body and make determinations. The body *has* a language. It talks. It can say, "I've had enough," or "I'll try a little more of that."

There are certain general commonsense pointers. If you haven't exercised in years, go slowly at first in every category. If you only weigh a hundred pounds, don't try to lift fifty your first session. If you have heart trouble, don't run or walk fast until you consult your physician.

Depending on your body condition, you may enter as an intermediate or even advanced, but I'm a believer in letting the exerciser judge his or her readiness to move on or stay put. If the beginning exercises in this book are all easy for you, then it is obvious that you should do more "reps," lift more weight; run, bike or swim longer. *Listen to your body and extend as it tells you.* But be patient with it, too. Whatever shape it is in happens to be your responsibility.

If the beginning exercises and routines aren't easy for you, then my advice, based on long experience, is *never, never* over-exercise; never exercise to the point that you're gasping for air. Never strain doing any of these exercises. Gradually build your level of fitness to the point where the exercises are easier. Little by little you'll be able to increase your stretch, lift more weights, run longer. When you over-exercise, your body becomes susceptible to injury, which could end up discouraging you from physical activity.

Every rule was made to be *wisely* broken, and aside from a few of the heavier weight lifts, every instruction herein is subject to variation. Each of us has a different capability, and if you can't perform all of the stretch, perform half of it. Set your own pace in doing each exercise. If you develop soreness in one part of the body or another, ease off; go slower. The slow and steady, persistent approach will lead to a better body.

Though I haven't mentioned sports in an advocate manner, it goes with the territory of this book to say that participation in tennis, racquetball, volleyball—any sport of your choosing—is, indeed, a plus for fitness, as well as a plus for fun.

There comes a point when I say to my new clients, "Let's see what you can do. Up on your toes, slowly, raise your arms in front of you slowly . . . find your balance . . . hey, stop wobbling around . . . c'mon, you can do it. . . ."

THE EXERCISES

11

BALANCE AND CONTROL

For general fitness, pleasing appearance, confidence and safety—for young and old.

Even the clumsiest of us are born with a sense of balance, striving for body control while still in the crib, eventually sitting up unaided, eventually walking, "doing what comes naturally" to control our feet, legs, arms and hands and then the entire movement of our bodies. But after the formative years—and sometimes during these years—we often drift into bad posture and clumsiness worsens. By old age, we slouch, slump and creak. We lose our sense of balance, and fall down and break bones. But it has more to do with pure laziness and muscle atrophy than the inner ear. Needless to say, bad "carriage" habits of early life tend to increase in later life. *Awareness*, at any and all stages, is the key to correction. By being aware of the body and how you carry it, you can make corrections at almost any age.

HOW?   *Special stretching exercises!*

WHEN?   Every single day.

TIPS   1. Easier without shoes, particularly balancing on toes.

2. Better in front of a mirror.

3. Go slow. No jerky movement.

4. Slowly increase the time of each stretch. Slowly! Slowly!

5. Feel your leg and thigh muscles as they give support; be aware of them; think about them as foundations.

6. Most of all, be aware and *see* your body alignment; stand sideways and look in the mirror, straighten posture while stretching; face the mirror, straighten posture while stretching. Shape up!

FOR: Gaining awareness of balance, body alignment.

1. Stand with feet slightly apart, arms at your sides, body erect and relaxed. Slowly rise up on your toes. Feel entire body lifting up toward ceiling.

2. Fully realize this position, making sure your balance is solid; then allow your head to slowly release back as far as it will go. Hold this position for several seconds, *without tension in the neck.*

3. Slowly bring your head back up to start position, while keeping your balance *up on your toes.*

4. Slowly release head forward as far as it will go (chin toward collarbone area). Hold for a second or two, then bring head back up and lower heels to the floor.

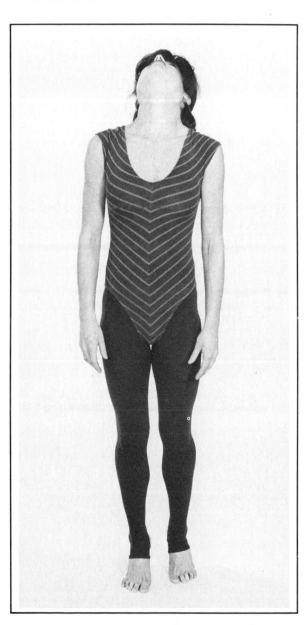

NOTE: **At first you can steady yourself by lightly touching a wall or other stationary object. Don't lean, just use it as an assist to help you find your balance.**

KNEE LIFT BALANCE

Balance
and Control

FOR: Legs, hips, awareness of balance.

1. Standing on one foot, slowly lift the other foot, bending knee upward to the waist. Arms are over your head, out to the side or down at your sides. Foot flexed or pointed.

2. With the leg up, hold 3 to 5 seconds, supporting your body with opposite thigh and buttock.

3. Work to keep your balance and your back straight and body centered. While holding, create the sensation of balance and control of your body in your mind's eye.

4. Then reverse with the opposite knee straight and the other knee bent to the waist.

Do 3 to 4 times on each leg, alternating.

VARIATION: Do the same exercise as above, only up on your toes. One leg first and then the other. Do 3 to 4 times on each leg, alternating.

NOTES:
1. **In the beginning, these can be done with some support from a nearby wall.**
2. **Tightening your buttocks will help you keep your balance.**
3. **Experiment with arm positions (even clasped behind head). Experiment with leg positions (leg straight in front, to the side or back).**

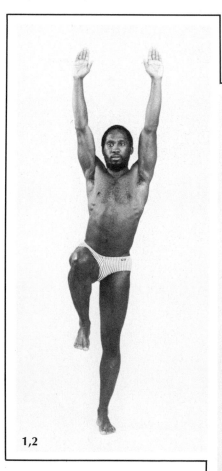

1,2

FOR: All-over body toner—especially hips, obliques (waist), rib cage, shoulders, balance and flexibility.

1. Standing on one foot, slowly bend knee upward to the waist. With hands clasped behind head, touch opposite elbow to waist-high knee. Reverse.

2. Do same exercise standing up on your toes. Do 5 times on each leg, alternating.

3. Standing on one foot, slowly bend knee upward, this time out to the side. With hands clasped behind head, touch same-side elbow to knee. Do 5 times. Reverse legs; do 5 times on the other side.

4. With arms out to the sides, and leg, raised, slightly bent in front of you, hold position for 5 seconds. Reverse legs.

NOTE: **Slowly. Each repetition should be done in one smooth move. No jerking or forcing your muscles.**

FORWARD LUNGE (Straight Leg)

Balance and Control

FOR: Improving balance and agility. Overall body toner, particularly hips, buttocks and thighs.

1. Rise onto your toes, extend one leg forward with toe pointed. Keep your balance on back foot. Arms out to the sides.

2. Lunge onto outstretched forward leg until the knee is fully bent, foot flat on floor. The opposite leg, extended straight behind, is supported on the toes. Knee should *not* touch the floor.

3. Balance for a second or two in the low lunge position.

4. To get back to your start position, lift body up as you push off from the front leg and onto the straight back leg—maintaining balance.

5. Bring front leg down so you are balanced on both feet—still up on your toes.

6. Start exercise again, raising opposite leg.

Do 2 or 3 times on each side.

NOTES:

1. **The only way to gain balance and body control is to practice it frequently, doing mental homework as well as physical. You must think about *centering* the body.**

2. **Throughout the exercise, arms should be extended straight out to the sides to assist balance.**

3. **This is not a jump. The foot you are balanced on as you begin lunge never leaves the floor.**

4. **Do these very slowly and with intention. See the lunge successfully completed; *intend* to accomplish it. If your body falls short of what is in your mind, don't fret, keep at it. In time your body will strengthen and gain the ability to support you in fulfilling what your mind intends.**

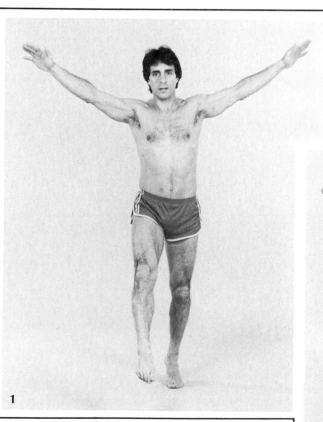

1

2,3

FOR: Improving balance and agility. Overall body toner, particularly hips, buttocks and thighs.

1. Raise yourself onto toes and lift one knee so that pointed toe reaches to the knee of standing leg, both knees facing forward. Arms out to the sides, shoulder level.

2. Balancing on one leg, extend bent leg straight in front.

3. Lift with the upper body and allow yourself to move forward in a controlled fall.

4. Land on a fully bent front leg, with the other leg straight in back, both heels off the floor. Hold position for a second or two.

5. "Push off" the forward, bent leg and lift your body back and up onto straight back leg—keeping front leg as high as possible and retaining balance.

6. Lower heels to floor. Raise onto toes again and do lunge on other leg.

Do 2 to 3 on each side.

VARIATION: Bend the raised leg to the side—and lunge out to the side using same form as for forward lunge.

NOTE: **Don't throw your body into lunges. Be careful not to overextend to a point that you lose control of your balance.**

BASIC BEND-BACK

Advanced
Balance and
Control

FOR: Creating a mental and physical awareness of balance and control. Total body conditioner.

1. Rise up on toes, knees locked, arms raised in front, body erect. Once you have "locked in" your balance, tighten your buttocks.

2. Slowly bend your knees, keeping them just a few inches apart (maintain this distance throughout exercise). A common tendency is to allow knees to go out to the sides; don't let this happen. Buttocks and hips support you. Raise arms for balance as you bend farther back.

3. Rise up out of bend-back position with the same form, control and at the *same* slow rate that you descended.

Do this one full time through.

NOTES:

1. **The purpose of this exercise is to assist you to develop control and balance, and at the same time stretch and strengthen many muscles of your body. It is to be done extremely slowly.**

2. **Throughout this exercise, keep your body from your head to your knees in one solid piece. No "sagging" in the middle, or "sitting" with the hips and buttocks, or arching too much with upper back or head. It is imperative to work for correct form and little by little increase the degree of the bend-back. Going very low but not in the proper form produces no benefit.**

3. **Do not be discouraged if at first you cannot accomplish this whole exercise with all its sequences. Keep at it; doing what you can and always striving to improve. I promise that you will . . . you must will your body and your balance and your control to do it.**

1

2

2a

FOR: Calves, fronts of thighs, buttocks, awareness of body alignment.

1. Begin sitting on the floor, one leg crossed over the other.

2. Shift your weight forward onto your front foot and rise slowly to your full height with your arms outstretched, elbows locked over your head.

3. Bring back leg across the front and reverse the exercise, slowly lowering yourself to cross-legged position on the floor. Or *slowly* pivot in place in the direction of the leg in back, shifting your weight onto opposite leg, lowering yourself to seated position with opposite leg bent over in front.

Do 3 to 4 repetitions on each side.

NOTES:

1. **Throughout exercise, concentrate on keeping your balance and moving in one continuous flow.**

2. **This exercise helps you discover what muscles it takes to accomplish coming up and going back down to the floor.**

3. **Be aware of: (a) what your muscles are doing, (b) how they need to be strengthened, (c) where the support comes from in raising and lowering yourself.**

12

STRETCHING

For general fitness and conditioning, reduction of muscle tension, flexibility, toning up particular areas of the body, warming up prior to cardiovascular exercise and specific sports such as tennis; circulation aids for ages five to ninety-five—or even more.

Whatever praise I've given stretching in the first part of this book is not praise enough. These unique exercises—replacing the jerking, bouncing, often harmful repetitions of yesteryear, the "push-up" and "sit-up" schools— are so versatile that I'm convinced we have yet to fully realize all the benefits to the body. Though they have become increasingly popular, they are not revolutionary in any sense. In fact, I think they are nature's safe way of exercising.

WHEN? Every day, and as applicable.

HOW? Use the general stretches for all-around fitness and conditioning; use the specific stretches as warm-ups prior to running, biking, tennis, etc.

TIPS 1. Take a warm bath or shower prior to stretching sessions to ease tight muscles and increase the flow of blood to them.

2. Wear comfortable clothing that "gives." My favorite is loose sweat

pants and loose sweat pullover. But what is comfortable to you is what counts.

3. Check the time when you begin. Set a goal, in minutes, that you can keep. Perhaps 15 minutes in the beginning; extending to 30 minutes; extending to 45 minutes. As you progress, you'll find you can take less time in completing a given set of exercises.

4. Atmosphere may or may not be needed, but it should be tried— music or TV. Some people prefer to work out in total silence and use the time to think; others need music; others watch the morning or evening news shows. Whatever supports your exercise session is what should be used.

5. Go ever so slowly. The whole idea of stretching is to be like a cat, to work the muscles slowly and luxuriously, not to bounce and batter them. If you only accomplish three sets of exercises within your beginning time frame, that's great. Those three will have benefited your body.

6. Total Breathing is an amazing power source while stretching, just as it is while lifting weights. An inhale, properly timed, may afford you that extra inch of stretch that you're seeking.

7. Stretching is a "thinking" exercise in that you should be aware of the particular muscles that are being utilized; "see" them beneath your skin as well as feel them.

8. No two days of stretching will be alike. You'll be "tighter" some days; there may be pockets of pain—work around them or skip that area of the body for that day. There may be soreness in the thighs or in the deltoids. Don't punish them. Stay in tune with your body while toning it. Massage it, mentally and physically.

I once had a client tell me, "I was going so slow, standing there and stretching, that I almost fell asleep."

"Great," I said.

TWO-WAY STRETCH or GOOD-MORNING STRETCH

Stretching

FOR: Aligning the spine and entire body, this stretch "wakes up" the body, eliminating sluggishness. Puts you in tune with your body, making you aware of and connected to it. Counteracts problems that may arise in the elbow region through the aging process of muscle shrinkage.

1. Standing with feet slightly apart, knees locked, body relaxed and erect, raise one arm (bending elbow and "unfolding" arm) close to your ear, up high overhead.

2. Keeping back straight, reach up toward the ceiling as the other arm stretches down toward the floor. Be sure your hands (with fingers very straight and lined up touching each other) are extensions of each arm without breaking at the wrist. Think of your arms as arrows and your hands as arrowheads, both going straight to their destinations—the ceiling and the floor.

3. *Inhale* as arm goes overhead and hold breath until you have stretched to your maximum. Hold for 2 to 5 seconds. Then *exhale* as you release arms from stretch.

4. Reverse, bending both elbows, and exchange direction of arms. The arm that was down now stretches upward and vice versa.

Do 3 to 5 times on each side.

VARIATION: This entire exercise can also be done while standing on your toes, keeping body straight and knees locked. This is a terrific "two for one" exercise in that it's an excellent stretch, while at the same time developing balance.

NOTES:

1. **This total body stretch can be done when you get up first thing in the morning (or even while lying in bed). Do this stretch several times a day to align and enliven your body.**

2. **Do this stretch before any physical activity. This should be the *first* exercise of your stretch workout.**

3. **Do this stretch after *every* lift with weights, for it keeps the muscles constantly supple, enlongated and counteracts the tightening that comes from certain lifting and resistance exercises.**

2 3   4   4a

FOR: Mobility in the neck and upper shoulder area, neckline and chin.

1. Slowly let your head relax forward; now roll to one side, continue to the back, to the other side and now forward again.

2. This is a very slow circle of the head in one continuous movement. Relax neck muscles and allow weight of head to determine the circling motion.

Do at least 4 circles in each direction.

NOTE: Move slowly. Do not force your neck muscles. Concentrate on relaxing that area throughout exercise.

SHOULDER ISOLATION

Stretching

FOR: Mobility in shoulder area, neck and shoulder blades.

1. Stand straight up with arms relaxed at your sides.

2. Lift one shoulder as high as you are able, letting arm hang relaxed, keeping body straight and centered. Lower shoulder; do 10 repetitions.

3. Do the same thing with other shoulder; 10 repetitions.

4. Lift both shoulders simultaneously; 10 repetitions.

5. Do entire sequence making "circles"—lift up, back, down and forward in one continuous circular motion. First with one shoulder, then the other and finally with both simultaneously. Reverse direction of circles. Do 10 repetitions each.

NOTE: **Keep shoulder and neck area relaxed. Do not jerk or tighten these muscles. Keep in mind the purpose is to make this often rigid area more flexible.**

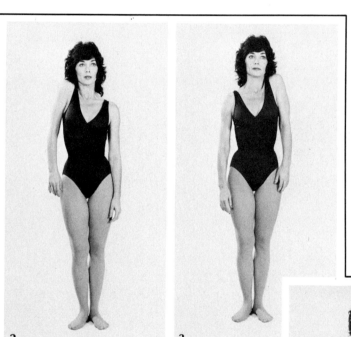

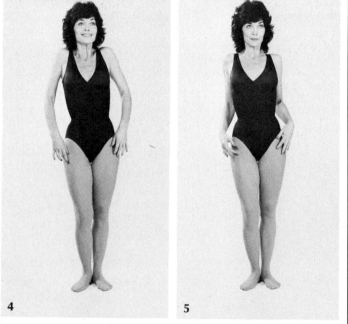

FOR: Upper back, shoulders and arms. Tones flabbiness under upper arms.

1. Stand straight with knees locked. Put arms straight out to the side at shoulder level with elbows locked and hands extended, fingers together.

2. Make circles 10 times in one direction, then stop.

3. Do 10 circles in the other direction.

Do at least 20 circles.

NOTES:

1. **At first do this exercise slowly and feel the circular motion. Start with small circles and gradually build up to larger ones. For instance: make the first 5 circles about 2 to 4 inches in diameter; the second 5 circles should increase in size to a maximum of 1 to 2 feet in diameter.**

2. **These go by very quickly, so feel free to increase the amount or even the patterns.**

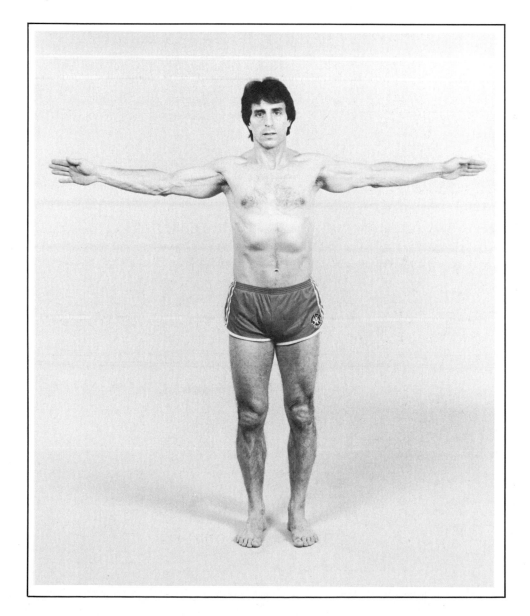

ARM ISOLATION

Stretching

FOR: Shoulders, deltoids, upper arms, elbows, wrists, hands, knees, calves and buttocks.

1. Stand with both knees bent (one only slightly more so than the other). One foot is placed flat on the floor and the other foot is out to the side and up on the toes.

2. Put one hand on your hip or down to your side.

3. "Isolate" the other arm—extend it out away from your body, elbow locked and rotate arm in one direction as far as possible. Then rotate it in other direction. During these moves, keep your hand in the same spot, so arm turns in its socket. Don't let arm flop around. Lock elbow—visualize the arm as one solid piece (a stick, pole, or whatever) that rotates from the shoulder and acts as an axle.

4. Hold each "arm turn" position for 5 seconds.

Do 4 or 5 arm turns (forward and back counts as 1 turn), then change sides and repeat whole sequence with other arm.

NOTE: **The idea is to "isolate" one arm at a time, moving only that arm and no other part of your body. Hold torso and legs very still as you work the arm.**

1 2

3 4

FOR: Waistline, upper body toning and body control.

1. Stand with legs comfortably apart, hands on hips. *Without swiveling hips* and *keeping the lower body stationary,* you are going to move the rib cage in several patterns. Think of the upper body as a separate unit, keeping the lower body firmly in position. Keep the knees locked at all times.

2. Move rib cage directly to the right as far as possible. Return to the start position, then reach to the left.

3. Move your rib cage forward as far as you can, then return to start position. Move rib cage back as far as possible, then return to start position. Repeat several times, relaxing in between.

4. Now do 4 repetitions in each direction (4 to the right side, 4 to the front, etc.); then do 2 repetitions each way; then 1 repetition. Reverse the whole pattern, starting to the left, then back, right and forward.

5. Now try "circling" the rib cage in one continuous move. Without stopping, move through all four directions in a smooth circular motion. Do at least 4 circles in both directions.

NOTE: Be adventurous; make up your own patterns.

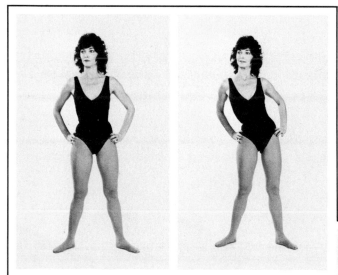

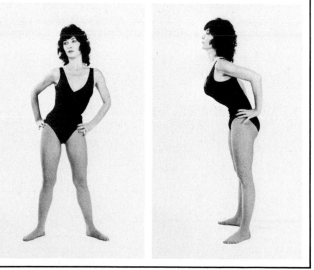

FLAT-FOOTED HALF SQUAT

Stretching

FOR: Buttocks, thighs, calves.

1. Stand with feet wide apart, heels on the floor and hands on hips.
2. Slowly bend knees and bring body to as low a squat position as possible, keeping heels on the floor.
3. Hold position for a second or two and then slowly come up, using buttocks and thighs to assist your ascent.

NOTES:
1. **Breathe in going down; exhale coming up.**
2. **Keep your back as straight and upright as possible.**

FOR: Hips, buttocks, waist, hamstrings, calves, lower back.

1. Start position is flat on soles of feet, arms extended overhead, elbows locked.

2. Bend from the hips and reach forward with torso and arms. Head up. Control bend with the buttocks.

3. When back is parallel to the floor, lower head so you are facing the floor. Intensify reach by stretching forward, but keeping your back straight.

4. Slowly come back up to start position.

Do 4 or 5 repetitions.   NOTE: **Keep legs straight throughout exercise.**

FULL CIRCLE REACH

Stretching

FOR: Waist, midsection, back, obliques (muscles on sides of waist that some-times distend—trouble spot for men).

1. Stand erect with legs comfortably apart, arms over head, elbows locked. Twist upper torso to one side.

2. Bend from hips, reaching out as far as you can (this stretches the oblique muscles).

3. Slowly bend further, continuing to reach. Make a circular pattern that sweeps down toward the floor then around to the other side—always reaching with your arms—out and up. Keep knees locked throughout.

4. Return to start position. Reverse direction and circle-stretch the other way.

Do 3 or 4 full circles in each direction.

NOTE: **Keep your breathing relaxed and natural all during the exercise.**

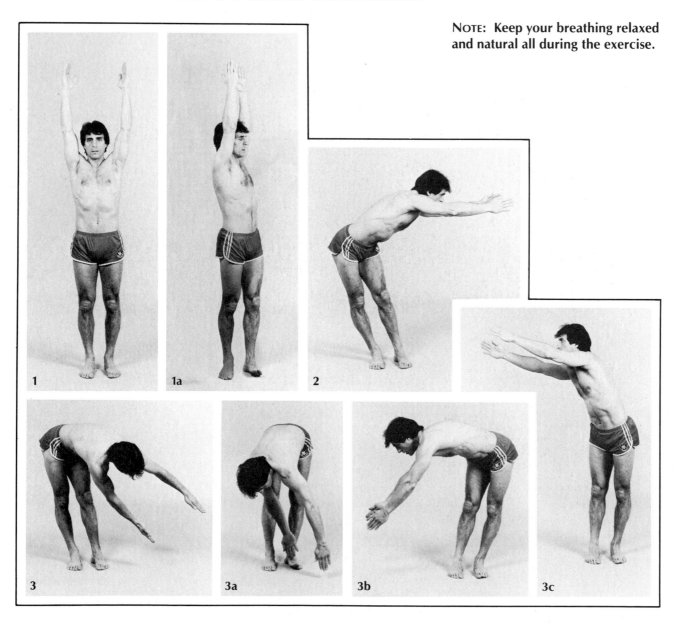

FOR: Waist and upper torso, obliques.

1. This is a variation of the Full Circle Reach, omitting the lower half of the stretch. Stand straight up, legs comfortably apart, arms extended over head. Stretch to one side, reaching out with both arms.

2. Bending from the hips, directly to the side, go to the point where your back is parallel to the floor. Constantly reach out, keeping knees locked.

3. Reverse the process. Come back to a standing position and do the exercise to the other side.

Do 3 or 4 times to each side.

NOTE: **Breathe naturally throughout exercise.**

JACKKNIFE STRETCH
(Locked Knees)

Stretching

FOR: Hamstrings, buttocks, backs of calves.

1. Stand with feet apart. Lock both knees and bend from the waist until body is parallel with one leg; grasp with both hands, placing head against leg. Hold for 3 to 5 seconds.

2. Still bent over, slowly shift upper torso to other leg. Grasp leg in both hands.

3. Then, place both elbows on the floor and hold for 3 to 5 seconds.

Do 2 to 3 repetitions.

NOTES:
1. **To be done slowly; a steady continuous stretch. No bouncing or jarring of the body.**

2. **Even if only your fingertips touch the floor, do not be discouraged. The model in these photographs is extremely and unusually limber. Just go as far as *you* can toward the floor—keeping knees straight. Stay with it, you will gradually become more limber and be able to go lower and lower.**

90

FOR: Groin, buttocks and thighs.

1. With legs spread far enough apart to enable you to put forearms on the floor, slowly start easing your legs into a split. Control the descent with turned-in feet.

2. As your legs widen out, lower your body until you are in a split with elbows fully bent and, if possible, on the floor.

3. If you are extremely flexible, entire torso can eventually be flat on the floor during split.

Do 2 to 4 repetitions.

NOTES:
1. **Again, go slowly. Do not attempt the full stretch until your body is limber enough.**
2. **If this exercise seems impossible, try this: with legs spread out to the sides, reach over with knees locked and touch floor with hands, then slowly lower your body, touching floor with wrists and finally forearms.**

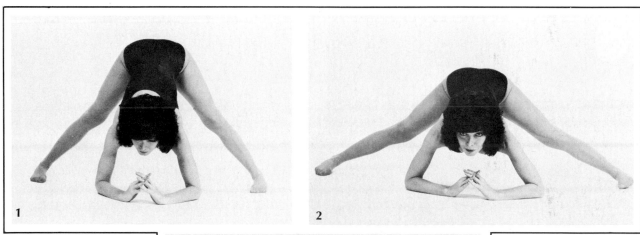

OBLIQUE STRETCH

Stretching

FOR: Obliques, sides of the waist ("handlebars" that plague many men).

1. Start with hands held behind buttocks, standing with feet apart, flat on the floor. Bend back slightly from the hips. Bend knees only slightly.

2. With elbow locked, reach with one arm to touch back of opposite knee with hand. Other arm bends slightly in the process.

3. Reverse sides, reaching with the other arm.

Do 10 to 15 repetitions on each side.

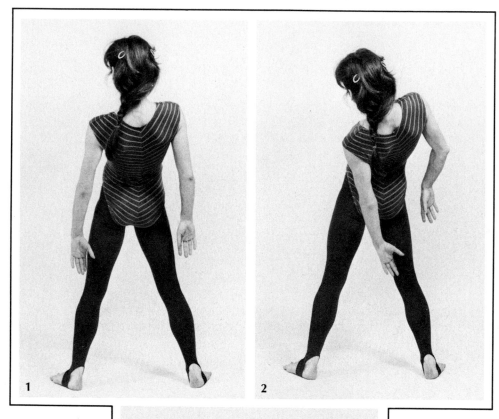

FOR: Chest, shoulders, abdomen, buttocks, hips, quadriceps and knees.

1. Place feet apart, flat on floor; bend knees.

2. With hands on hips, slowly bend back.

NOTES:

1. **Be sure to proceed slowly with control. Go as far back as your body will allow without forcing or jerking. Do not go back to a point where you are unable to control returning to a standing position.**

2. **Keep buttocks firm throughout exercise. This is your source of support.**

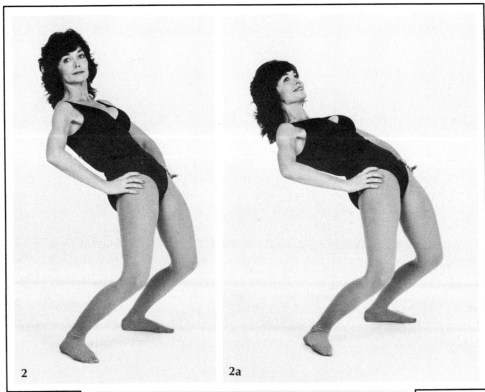

2

2a

2b

WALL KNEE LIFTS

Stretching

FOR: Toning thighs, buttocks and hips.

1. Stand straight with your back placed against a smooth-surfaced wall.

2. Slowly lower your body until you're in a "sitting" position that you can sustain. Your back against the wall will support you. Keep both feet flat on the floor.

3. Balancing on one leg, with your back still pressed against the wall, lift one leg, knee bent as high as comfortably possible. Hold knee up for 3 to 5 seconds.

4. Slowly lower leg and repeat exercise with opposite leg.

Do 2 or 3 times on each leg.

VARIATION: In step 3, straighten leg. Flex foot, then point. Repeat. Switch legs.

NOTES:

1. **Your breathing can help you sustain the performance of this exercise. Take regular deep breaths—inhaling and exhaling evenly.**

2. **You may use your arms against the wall for support.**

3. **Don't go so low into the sitting position that you have trouble getting back up. If you ever feel you are "stuck" and can't seem to get up, use your arms and hands to push off wall and just walk straight ahead.**

4. **If you need to rest, stand up between knee lifts for a moment, then resume exercise.**

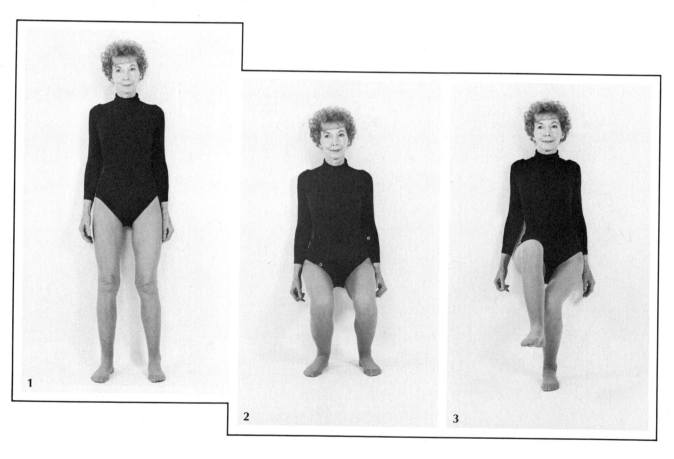

FOR: Hips, thighs, outer thighs and rib cage.

1. From a kneeling position, with arms up overhead, slowly lower body to one side as if to sit down—don't sit!

2. Go sideways as far as possible, feeling the stress on the hip and buttocks area.

3. When you have gone as low to the floor as possible without sitting, hold the position for a moment.

4. *Slowly* rise up out of position and in one continuous move, flow through the start position and repeat the exercise on the opposite side.

Do 3 to 5 times on each side.

VARIATIONS: Start with your arms outstretched at shoulder level, straight in front. Move them to the opposite side from the leaning hips.

NOTE: I started this exercise for skiers but it works just as well for those who don't ski. Stresses hips!

SKI TURN
(Arms
Overhead)

Stretching

SOLE-TO-SOLE SIDE STRETCH

Stretching

FOR: Groin, rib cage, obliques.

1. Assume semi-lotus position—soles of feet flush together. Both knees as close to the floor as possible and heels as close into groin as you are able.

2. Facing forward, lean upper body to one side. Holding toes to keep feet in position, fold arm under torso and reach head toward knee.

3. At the same time, hold other knee down with hand—this provides maximum stretch. Hold position for 3 to 5 seconds.

4. Come up to start position and bend to the other side.

Do 2 to 3 repetitions on each side.

1

2 3

FOR: Groin, legs, back.

1. Sit on the floor with legs together, extended in front of you.

2. Bend one knee, grasp foot and place it on the opposite thigh as close to the crotch as possible. This is a half lotus. Be careful not to overstretch.

3. Bend the other leg, lifting foot over opposite calf onto thigh. Be sure your back is straight. This is a full lotus.

Sit in this position for 30 to 60 seconds at first, gradually increasing your time in this stretch.

NOTES:
1. **Be sure your back is straight, lifting with your abdomen.**

2. **Do not overstretch.**

3. **This is a stretch you must develop gradually. The more you do it, the more limber you'll become.**

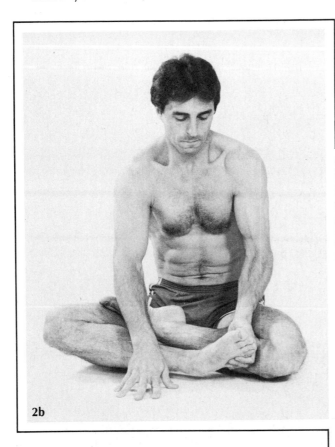

2b

3

WRAPAROUND STRETCH

Stretching

FOR: Entire torso, latissimus dorsi ("lats"), hips and thighs.

1. Begin in sitting position, one leg tucked under you and the other crossed over with foot flat on the floor.

2. Reach both arms overhead and stretch up and out over front leg without rising from seating position. Hold for 3 to 5 seconds.

3. Bring arms back down and extend at shoulder level away from crossed leg—turning torso from the waist at the same time arms reach back. Hold for 3 to 5 seconds.

4. Bend arm nearest knee and exert a slow steady pressure against thigh, which enables torso to turn even more. Hold for 3 to 5 seconds.

5. Come back to facing front again and repeat exercise.

Do 3 repetitions, then change legs and do 3 repetitions on the other side.

NOTE: Derived from the yoga discipline, this exercise should be done slowly with a continuous flow of movement, not bounces, pulses or jarring force.

1 2

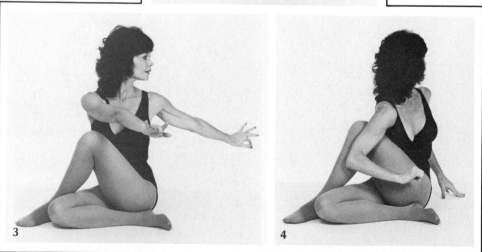

3

4

FOR: Entire leg, especially the back of the leg (Achilles tendon and hamstrings), arms, shoulders, back and abdomen.

1. Sitting with knees bent to chest, hands holding toes, unfold one leg until it is straight forward with knee locked if possible (go forward as far as your body will allow).

2. Then as you come back to the starting position, stretch the other one forward as far as can be extended.

3. Then do the same action with both legs simultaneously. As flexibility increases, put elbows on floor while holding toes.

Do 4 repetitions on each leg.

NOTE: **This exercise should help those who haven't enough flexibility to touch their hands to their toes.**

SEATED REACH

Stretching

FOR: Back, hips, thighs, flexibility.

1. Start in a seated position, legs extended, knees locked, toes pointed. Stretch arms fully above head.

2. Let head relax back as far as possible as hands reach for the ceiling.

3. Bring outstretched arms forward, elbows locked, keeping back as straight as you can.

4. Continue reaching out past your feet, with head up, until hands are on the floor, torso against thighs.

5. Grasp ankles and bring forehead down to legs. Hold 3 to 5 seconds.

6. Then raise back up to sitting position using stomach muscles, not lower back.

Do 4 repetitions.

100

FOR: Groin, lower back, thighs and abdomen; increased flexibility.

1. Sit with your legs out as far as possible to the sides, knees facing the ceiling and feet flexed or pointed.

2. Put your hands on the floor behind buttocks, keeping knees locked.

3. While breathing out, bend over slowly from the waist, reaching down and forward with your forehead while extending arms up over your head and out in front of you. Hold this position a second or two. *Remember*—work up to this stretch gradually.

4. Inhale while straightening to upright position.

Do 3 or 4 stretches forward—remaining in split position—going a little lower to the floor each time.

NOTES:
1. **Do this exercise without any jarring motions; just slowly move forward in your stretch as far as you can.**
2. **Be sure to spread your legs *only* as far as they will go. Do not strain.**

LATERAL SPLIT STRETCH II

Stretching

FOR: Groin, hips, thighs, lower back; increased flexibility.

1. Sit on the floor with your legs as far apart as possible, still allowing yourself to sit up straight with knees locked, hands in front to help lift the back.

2. Reach right arm up and over your head and stretch directly sideways over the left leg. Left arm rests on the floor in front of you.

3. Come up slowly, reverse arms and repeat on opposite side.

4. With legs still spread, put palms in front of you flat on the floor (to control the amount of stretch to the groin) and bring chest down to the floor keeping your back straight. As flexibility increases, you will come from sitting in the split position forward on your palms to a lying down split position with forearms on the floor. This move is accomplished with groin area very close to the ground.

Do entire exercise 4 times.

NOTE: Breathe naturally throughout exercise; find your own breath pattern that supports your workout.

FOR: Obliques, waist, lats, arms. Aids the "handlebars" that are troublesome for some men.

1. Sit on the floor with legs wide, knees locked.

2. Supporting upper body with one arm behind you, incline body back and to that side.

3. Keeping both feet on the floor, lock elbow of other arm and raise arm to eye level. Twisting your body, sweep arm across and down as far as you can go, touching floor if possible. Opposite leg may raise off floor a bit; supporting arm can bend. Hold for a second or two.

4. Without stopping, in one slow continuous movement, bring outstretched arm back and lean on it, then reach across with other arm to the other side.

Do 6 to 10 reaches on each side, alternating arms.

2 3

4

SEATED LEG STRETCH

Stretching

FOR: Groin, thigh area, balance and body control.

1. Sit with both knees bent fully and drawn in close to body (à la "cannonball" position).

2. Extend one leg, knee locked and toe pointed. Pull bent knee of other leg back as far as possible—past torso if you are able.

3. Repeat this with other leg.

4. Now do the same stretch with extended leg bent in halfway.

5. Repeat this with other leg.

6. Now, holding heels and keeping your balance, extend one leg up and out to the side as high as it will go.

7. Repeat this with other leg.

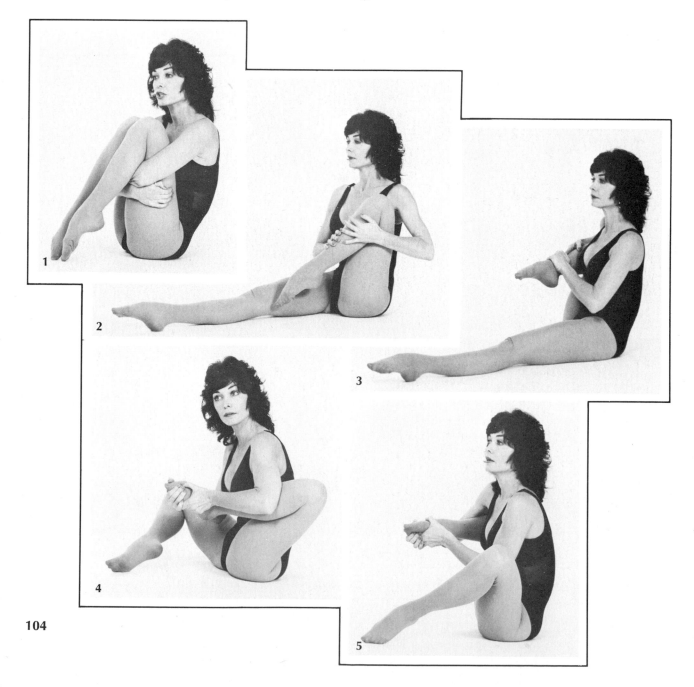

8. Now, do this last stretch with both legs opening simultaneously. Concentrate. Find your balance and hold for a few seconds. Be careful not to collapse over backward. If you do, simply round your back and roll gently back onto the floor.

9. Close to first position.

Do entire exercise (all 8 sequences) at least 1 or 2 times. You will need to do more repetitions of latter sequence (extended leg balance) in order to master it.

NOTE: **These are flexibility and leg control exercises that put medium to high stress on the knee, groin and thigh areas, from a sitting position. During exercise, keep back as straight and body as upright as possible. It should be done slowly, with control.**

6

7

8

8a

9

YOGA STRETCH SEQUENCE

Stretching

FOR: Groin, thigh, knee, calf, ankle, feet and back.

1. Start sitting on the floor, legs directly in front of you, knees locked, toes pointed. Throughout exercise, work to keep your back straight and your upper body upright, centered and under control. Even though you may not be able to accomplish this at first, the best benefit comes from doing this exercise properly.

2. Bend one knee to the side, supporting foot with one or both hands underneath ankle. Bring heel into the groin area (foot resting on other thigh) as far as you can. From this position, lower bent knee while mentally visualizing your leg parallel to and flush on the floor. (Eventually, you will get there!) Try to achieve this downward stretch without using your hands to press knee to floor—but if you need the assistance, do so. Hold "down" position for a couple of seconds.

3. Release foot, supporting yourself or extending arms to the sides for balance, and slowly move the leg ("unfold" it) until it is straight out to the side as far as possible. Hold leg about 12 inches or so off the floor, toes pointed.

4. In this leg-extended position slowly flex foot, then point toe again; flex, point.

5. While still out to the side, rotate extended leg from the hip socket until it is as "turned in" (opposite of ballet dancers "turnout") as you can manage. Keeping leg straight and toes pointed, slowly bring leg, knees locked, straight in front of you, maintaining "turn in" and distance from the floor.

6. When leg is directly out in front of you, simultaneously flex foot and rotate leg so that it is no longer turned in. Lower leg to the floor. Repeat on opposite side.

NOTE: This exercise should be done very slowly and with a lot of intention—fully seeing and realizing the stretch as it takes place. Keep your body centered and erect throughout exercise. Increased flexibility, strength and the formation of muscles that have been virtually dormant are among the benefits provided by this exercise.

LOTUS FRONT AND BACK STRETCH

Advanced Stretching

FOR: Thighs, groin, abdomen, knees, ankles and lower back.

1. Assume lotus position.

2. Now round your back and slowly roll spine backward onto the floor, lowering your body into a lying-down position. Lower body stays in the lotus, knees pointing to the ceiling. If necessary, use your elbows, arms and hands to lower your torso to the floor.

3. Place hands on knees or on the floor. Maintain lotus, bringing legs toward your chest as far as possible. Hold a few seconds.

4. Slowly lower legs (still in lotus) from chest area until they are flat on the floor. You are now lying on your back in lotus position. Keep your back down on floor as much as you can. Be patient if you cannot achieve this position right away. In time, as flexibility increases through consistent workouts, you'll be amazed at what you can do.

5. Still lying down (or sitting up), come out of lotus position. Rest legs and groin area for about 5 to 10 seconds. Then get into lotus position with other leg crossed on top.

6. Using arms and hands for support and balance, come up forward onto your knees.

7. Controlling the degree of stretch by holding yourself on your forearms, slowly lower your body down toward the floor until you are lying completely flat with chest, abdomen, pelvic area and legs (still in lotus) touching the floor. Hold for a few seconds.

8. From this position—supported by your forearms—lift your head and upper body, keeping pelvis on the floor.

9. Lying on stomach, disengage legs from lotus position and rest groin for a moment.

Do one time through.

NOTE: Be patient and gentle with your body. No forcing—you could "pull" something.

PLOW WITH VARIATIONS

Stretching

FOR: Overall body stretch and tone, *especially the back*. Also, shoulders, abdomen, buttocks, legs through the toes. Developing balance and control.

1. Do a shoulder stand. Supporting your back with your hands, balance on your neck, shoulders and upper arms. Extend both legs straight up toward the ceiling. Body from shoulder to toes should be in a straight line. Realize position. Hold for a second or two.

2. Bend knees as you slowly take hands away from back, keeping your balance. Bring knees down to touch forehead. Hold for a second. Then extend legs straight back over your face, toes pointed. Hold for a second or so.

3. Slowly spread legs as wide as possible—with arms out to the sides on the floor or with hands on the small of your back for support.

4. Slowly move hands to clasp each ankle or shin. Increase outward leg stretch, going out a little wider. Hold for a second or two.

5. Bring legs back in, slowly bending knees till they touch forehead. From there, twist torso turning knees to one side.

6. Slowly lower knees over one shoulder, touching the floor with knees. Then extend both legs as far to the side as you can. Lock knees; hold for a second. Touch toes to floor (keeping legs together). A variation is to straighten only one leg.

(Continued on following page)

PLOW WITH VARIATIONS

Stretching

7. Bend knees, bringing legs back to center, knees to forehead. Then do the same thing to the other side.

8. Bend your knees, twist your torso and return to center. Keep buttocks lifted, back as straight as you can.

9. Extend both legs, toes touching the floor right over your head. From there (with legs straight) roll your back—one vertebra at a time—onto the floor (feel like a jackknife). Keep your legs extended and toes pointed until legs are perpendicular to floor.

10. From this point, slowly raise your head first and then your back up off the floor, lowering your legs only enough so you can reach them with straight extended arms. Flex your feet and touch fingertips to toes. Hold for 2 to 5 seconds or longer.

11. Lower your legs slowly and then bend forward touching forehead to legs.

Do one time very slowly, then build as your flexibility increases.

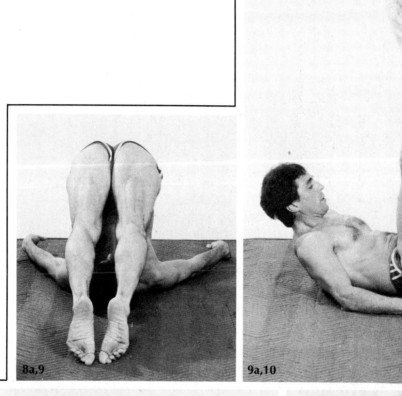

8a,9

9a,10

10a

11

SIDE PULL-UPS I

Stretching

FOR: Upper and lower abdomen and thighs.

1. Start position is prone, with arms extended above your head.
2. Raise arms, then head and shoulders up off the floor.
3. At the same time, lower your arms and bend knees into your body, turning them to the side away from your arms.
4. Extend arms, both at the same level, alongside torso and past thigh area. Hold this position for 3 to 5 seconds.
5. *Slowly* return to start position.

Do 3 to 4 repetitions on each side.

NOTES:
1. **Throughout entire exercise, be sure feet and arms do not touch the floor.**
2. **Maintain your balance coming up, holding position, and going back down to starting position.**
3. **Be sure to come up as far as possible in tucked position using your abdominal and buttocks muscles.**
4. **Breathe in coming up and exhale going back down.**

FOR: Upper and lower abdomen and thighs.

1. Start position is prone with arms extended to the sides.

2. Raise arms, legs, then head and shoulders up off the floor.

3. Bend knees up toward your body, twisting knees and torso in opposite directions.

4. Arms should be extended at shoulder level with the outside of the elbow touching the outside of the opposite knee. This position should be held for 3 to 5 seconds.

5. Slowly return to start position.

Do 3 to 4 repetitions on each side.

NOTES:

1. Be sure feet and arms do not touch the floor.

2. Maintain your balance while coming up, holding the position and going back down to start position.

3. Be sure to come up as far as possible in tucked position using your abdominal and buttocks muscles.

4. Breathe in coming up and exhale going back down.

SCISSOR STRETCH

Stretching

FOR: Defining the thighs and abdomen.

1. Start prone, knees locked, toes pointed, hands under buttocks. Elevate legs slightly.

2. Keeping legs a few inches off floor, open them out as far as possible, staying close to the floor. Hold for a second.

3. Return legs, still elevated, to parallel position. Keeping knees absolutely locked, cross feet four times—right over left, left over right, etc. Open legs as little as possible. It helps to turn legs out so heels lead the crossing action.

Do 10 or more repetitions.

NOTES:
1. **Heels should *not* touch the floor.**
2. **Slowly—no jerking legs apart or working from momentum.**

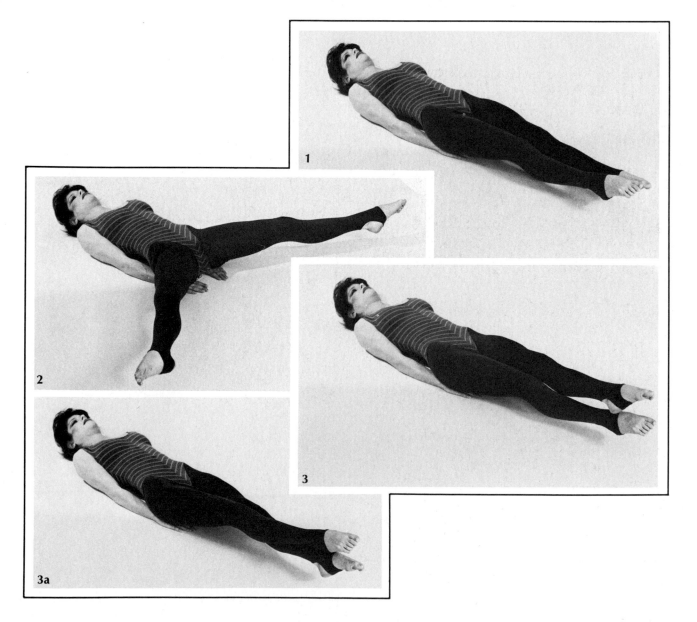

FOR: Thighs and buttocks, back, shoulders and arms.

1. Prone on the back, arms out to the sides, extend one leg straight up toward ceiling and cross over the other as high as possible (above waist if you can).

2. With foot flexed or pointed, touch the floor with the toes. Keep body centered as much as possible.

3. Bring leg back up to center position, then lower slowly to the floor.

4. Do the same thing with the other leg.

Do 3 to 5 repetitions on each leg, alternating sides.

VARIATION: Grasp foot or ankle of raised leg with opposite hand and pull leg across body.

NOTE: Excellent stretch comes from "turning-in" working leg from the hip socket through exercise. This may seem unachievable, but work for it mentally and physically.

FROG STRETCH

Stretching

FOR: Groin, thighs, hips, lower back, abdomen. Very good for hip flexibility.

1. Lie on back, legs lifted, knees open to the sides, soles touching, head on floor or lifted up.

2. Grasp ankles. Draw feet into groin area while gently pressing knees down toward the floor as much as possible.

3. Extend straight legs out as far as possible. Flex feet, point, stretch as much as you can; slow steady pressure from hands, not bouncing. Hold for a few seconds.

4. Let go of legs. Turn legs in *from the hip* and slowly bring legs together.

5. Keep legs turned in until they touch. Keeping legs off the floor, begin exercise again.

Do 4 or 5 repetitions.

VARIATION: In step 5, when legs are almost touching, lift one slightly above the other and cross. Then cross the other leg on top.

NOTE: **Control legs with abdomen, not the small of your back.**

FOR: Hips and outer thighs. This is a very effective technique for toning up the "saddle bag" or "upper thigh bump" area that plagues many women.

1. Lying on your back, bend both knees in toward your body.

2. Put one thigh down on the floor; point the knee of the other leg toward the ceiling.

3. Anchor the foot of the working leg behind the knee of the bottom leg.

4. Put one hand on raised knee, other hand on toes of bottom leg.

5. As your one hand slowly presses knee down toward the floor, the same leg resists. Your other hand steadies the rest of your body by clasping foot of bottom leg.

6. As your knee touches the floor, thigh continues resistance and pushes against hand on the way up. Go as slowly coming up as going down. Don't give up the resistance.

Do 3 or 4 repetitions on each side.

NOTE: **This exercise has the quality of a game in that the hand "wins" pushing the knee down against resistance and then the knee "wins" pushing up to start position overcoming resistance of the hand. You should feel the muscles in hips, buttocks and thighs really working; otherwise you are not doing this exercise properly.**

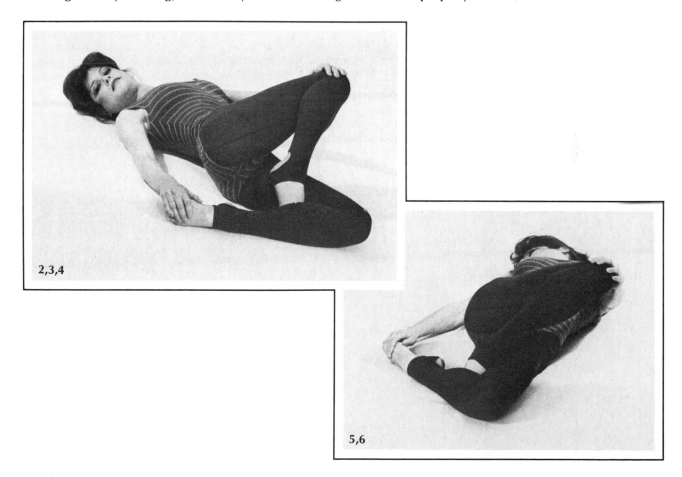

2,3,4

5,6

AROUND THE WORLD

Stretching

FOR: Total body conditioning—particularly the abdomen, thighs and buttocks.

1. Lie on back, arms extended to the sides, anchoring your body. Knees must be locked at all times and toes pointed throughout exercise except when directed to flex foot.

2. Slowly lift legs up toward ceiling until they are perpendicular to the floor.

3. Slowly lower legs to one side (keeping back on floor), until they are 3 to 4 inches from floor. Keep feet close to the floor, *but not touching it*. Legs extended fully, begin making a big half circle. Slowly bring legs past the center position and around to the other side, to waist level. Bring them up perpendicular to the floor, toes pointing at the ceiling.

4. Flex heels and slowly lower legs straight down to start position *almost* to the floor.

5. Without touching floor point toes, raise legs, and begin exercise again, this time circling in the other direction.

6. Bring legs slowly down to floor.

To start, do 1 circle in each direction. Quickly advance to multiple sets (3 or 4 sets, 6 or 8 circles).

NOTES:

1. As you circle, you must turn legs from hips while keeping shoulders and back flat on the floor—arms giving you support.

2. Keep both legs (hips and toes) in one solid line throughout exercise (as if it were "one leg").

3. Work to keep as much of your back *on* the floor as possible.

4. *Breathe!* Breath support will help you through some difficult spots during this exercise.

5. *Go very very slowly,* controlling every second.

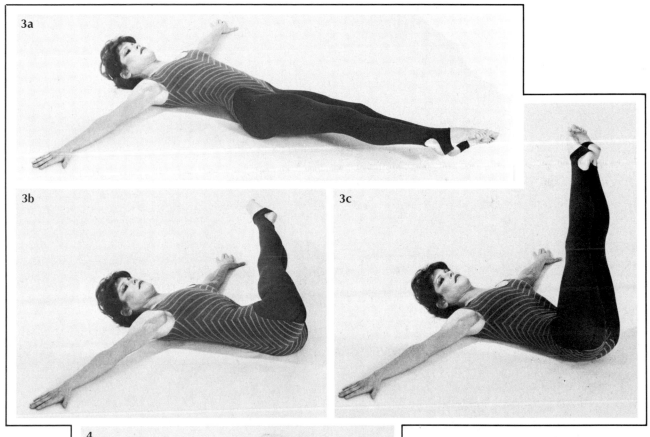

3a

3b

3c

4

CLIMB THE POLE For: Lower back, abdomen, thighs, buttocks.

Stretching

1. Lying on the floor, one knee bent, raise other leg straight up to ceiling at a 90-degree angle from the floor. Knee should be locked and toe pointed.
2. Grasp elevated leg at thigh with both hands, raising head and shoulders off the floor.
3. From this position "walk" the hands up the leg; bring your back off the floor.
4. Pull torso as parallel to the leg as possible.
5. Then slowly lower yourself to prone position and do same thing with other leg.

Do 2 to 3 repetitions on each side.

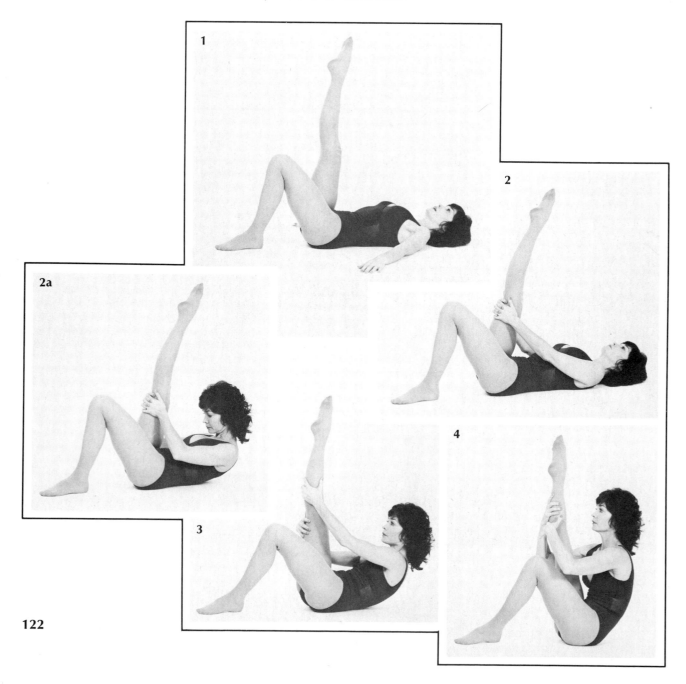

FOR: Entire leg, buttocks and hips.

1. Start position is on your side, supporting upper body with forearm and palm. Body and legs in one straight line, knees locked, toes pointed.

2. Raise top leg to a bent-knee position.

3. Slowly extend leg straight up toward the ceiling.

4. Slowly flex foot, then point foot and return to bent-knee position.

5. Move bent knee a little closer to your shoulder. From this new position extend leg to straight position *without moving knee*. In other words, hip to knee remains absolutely stationary as calf section of leg—knee to toe—extends out. Flex. Point. Return to bent-knee position.

6. Again move the bent knee a bit closer toward your body. Hold position a moment or two, then extend leg toward ceiling. Flex. Point. Return to start position.

7. Turn on your other side and repeat with other leg.

Do 6 to 10 repetitions on each side.

NOTES:
1. **Start with just the first 4 steps. Gradually build up to the Advanced part of the exercise (steps 5 & 6).**

2. **Gauge distance you bring your knee in so you don't move it too far in on the first few repetitions—leaving yourself nowhere to go. Eventually, knee will come up past your shoulder and foot will extend beyond your head.**

LEG LIFT
(Back)

Stretching

FOR: Toning buttocks, thighs and stomach.

1. Lying on stomach, legs extended, supporting body on elbows, lock the knees and slowly raise and lower legs, one at a time, alternately.

Do 6 to 10 lifts on each leg.

NOTE: **Go up and down at the same rate—*very slowly!* Feel muscles working in buttocks and hips.**

1a

1b

13

WEIGHT LIFTING

For added strength, endurance, stamina, flexibility and posture; coordination, appearance (replacement of flab), toning up various parts of the body, self-confidence—for children and mothers and fathers and grandmothers and grandfathers. For everyone!

As the above indicates, I'm a total and complete advocate of weight training, with *free weights*. They are second only to stretching as all-around conditioners, and superior to stretching in terms of added strength and in isolating various parts of the body for tone-up—buttocks, abdomen, underarm flab. You choose the part, and there is a weight exercise to match.

WHEN? No more than every other day. Your muscles need to rest after a weight training session. *Do not train with weights daily.*

HOW? You must *carefully* learn how. I have some commandments on weight lifting:

Thou shalt lift with thy legs and buttocks, not thy lower back.

Thou shalt lift in the proper form, no matter how light the weight.

Thou shalt learn the proper form by lifting with a ''bare'' bar.

TIPS 1. *Weights have no brains. You must think for them.* While weights, lifted properly, are safe, I still caution about the *handling* of weights.

They are heavy objects and not to be lightly regarded during lifts, while changing disks on the bar or moving them about the bench or room. Injury can result from carelessness or improper lifting.

2. Before a lift using a barbell:

   a. Check to make sure weights are of the correct poundage and equal in weight on both ends of the bar. Do not have 10 pounds on one end and 20 on the other.

   b. Be certain that the collars securing the disks are tight. If the disks slide off one end, injury may result.

   c. Look around you to make certain you have enough room for the lift without danger of hitting anyone. Be sure there is no danger of harming someone in case you have to drop the weights.

3. Your mental attitude is as important as your physical attitude. It must involve *concentration* as well as *determination*. I believe that you should actually "see" the weight lifted before you lift it. The bar is on the floor or bench rack; you should visualize it going up, then perform the lift. As you execute the lift, your mind should be constantly coaching your body: "lift with the legs, feel the lifting occurring . . ." Heavy lifts demand great concentration, and the beginner should start with the same concentration with light lifts.

4. Between sets of lifts, always do the "lift" stretches to keep muscles flexible and lengthened, preventing them from bunching up.

   a. Two-Way Stretch

   b. Standing Bend-Back

   c. Shoulder Isolation

5. After short reps of stretches, walk around for 30 seconds to one minute.

6. Your rest period between stretches and lifts, for a recommended 2 minutes, should be relaxed and quiet, but not supine. I suggest just sitting still somewhere for 2 minutes.

Every weight lifter has his or her own program but mine is as follows:
- Set of lifts
- Three stretches
- Walk around for one minute
- Rest period
- Repeat set of lifts
- Repeat all above as long as you continue the weight workout

FOR: Arms, shoulders (deltoids), chest, entire torso (including abdomen; bust line for women).

Use lightweight dumbbells to begin with (3 to 5 pounds). When you are able to handle these, move up to the next weight (8 to 10 pounds).

1. Stand with your back straight, feet comfortably apart, knees locked.
2. Extend dumbbells directly out in front of you at shoulder level. From this position, you begin your circle.
3. *Inhale,* and in one slow continuous move take the dumbbells up over your head, out to the sides (as wide out as possible). As you continue moving dumbbells downward, *exhale* and bring them as low in front of you as you can, then bring them up to start position.
4. Reverse circle—*inhale* and extend dumbbells down, out, around up overhead, back to start position.

Do 10 to 12 repetitions—5 or 6 circles one direction, then 5 or 6 in the other direction.

NOTES:
1. **Keep your elbows locked throughout entire exercise.**
2. **The only part of you moving should be your arms. Get the sense of reaching out, away from body throughout the exercise.**

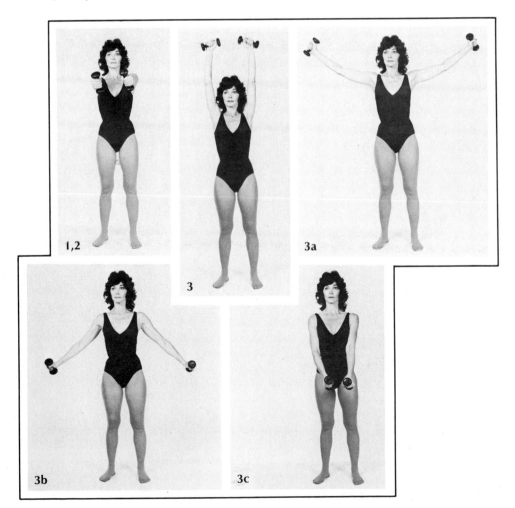

1,2

3

3a

3b

3c

DUMBBELL CLEAN AND SIMULTANEOUS PRESS

Weight
Training

FOR: Arms, shoulders, upper body strength.

1. *Clean* dumbbells: inhale as you lift them from the floor in one continuous movement, bringing them to slightly above each shoulder. Pause as you exhale.

2. Quick breath in and *press* both dumbbells straight up over your head. Elbows are locked and at the sides of your head.

3. Return to shoulder position and repeat press.

Do 6 to 8 repetitions of the press.

NOTE: Start with 5- or 10-pound dumbbells. Use larger ones as you become stronger. Be sure to keep dumbbells at the same height going up and down.

VARIATIONS: Dumbbell clean and alternate press.

1. To strengthen a weak arm, press only *one* dumbbell overhead, leaving the other in the shoulder (clean) position.

2. Reverse this move: as the arm doing the press starts down to the shoulder position, the other arm simultaneously starts a press.

3. Alternate.

Do 6 to 8 repetitions with each arm, or concentrate on one.

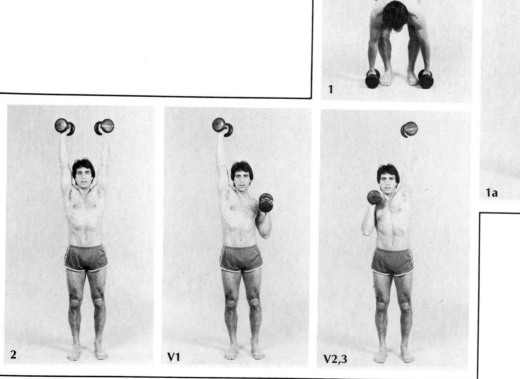

FOR: Overall toning and body conditioning that enhances balance and control.

1. Elevate on toes, arms extended with a 5-pound dumbbell in each hand.
2. Slowly bend knees, then slowly arch back, with buttocks tightly cupped, using weights as a counterbalance and point of focus.
3. Bend as far back as possible, keeping yourself locked in form.
3a. Slowly come back up to start position.
4. Lower heels to floor. Prepare to repeat with intention, then repeat.

Do 6 to 8 repetitions.

NOTES:
1. **Breathe in going back and exhale coming back to start position.**
2. **Stay within the form, don't let your knees go out to the sides. Pretend there's a vise on the outside of each knee, preventing them from spreading.**

DUMBBELL CROSS

Weight Training

FOR: Shoulders, neck and arms; particularly the back of the upper arm. This exercise does wonders for flab under the arms; tones up support muscles of the breasts (for women) and the chest (for men). Good for the entire upper body.

Use 3- to 5-pound dumbbells to begin with, heavier ones (up to 15 pounds) later on.

1. Sitting cross-legged, back and upper torso erect, extend dumbbells directly in front of you with elbows locked. Hold dumbbells end to end, parallel to the floor.

2. Inhale and slowly open arms out to the sides making sure you keep dumbbells steady, lined up and at shoulder level. Hold for a second.

3. Exhale as you slowly bring your arms back in toward each other. Maintain height and alignment of dumbbells.

4. In front of you, cross dumbbells one over the other as far as you can keeping arms straight. Return to start position.

5. Inhale and start exercise again; open out, hold, return back in, this time crossing the opposite arm over the other.

6. Using legs and buttocks, rise up out of the cross-legged position, still holding the weights.

Do 20 to 24 repetitions making sure you alternate crossing arms.

NOTE: **Keep arms and dumbbells absolutely straight and at shoulder level.**

For: Shoulders, bust line, arms. Great for toning under- and back-of-the-arm
flab.

Use 3- to 5-pound dumbbells—heavier as you advance in your weight training.

1. Sitting cross legged, back and upper torso erect, extend dumbbells directly
   in front of you with elbows locked. Hold dumbbells end to end, parallel
   to the floor.

2. Inhale and slowly open arms out to the sides, raised up above shoulder
   level to a V position. Hold for a second.

3. Exhale as you slowly bring your arms back in toward each other. Maintain
   height and alignment of dumbbells.

4. In front of you, cross dumbbells one over the other as far as you can
   keeping arms straight. Return to a starting V position.

5. Inhale and start exercises again; open out, hold, return back in, this time
   crossing the opposite arm over the other.

Do 20 to 24 repetitions.

Notes:
1. **Breathe in going out to sides and exhale coming in.**
2. **Be sure to keep dumbbells in same position you see in photo or else you'll end
   up banging them into each other.**

BENT ARM DUMBBELL PULLOVER

Weight
Training

FOR: Pectorals ("pecs"), chest, shoulders and arms.

Dumbbell should weigh amount you can handle—5 to 10 pounds for a beginner. This exercise can be done with bench flat.

1. Lie on bench. Hold dumbbell by one end in both your hands with your elbows bent. Hold dumbbell between 4 and 8 inches above your chest.
2. Inhale as you slowly move dumbbell along above your head and back down toward the floor. When you have extended your arms back as far as possible, hold for a moment.
3. Then exhale and bring dumbbell back in the same way you lowered it, up to start position.

Do 6 repetitions per set. Do 1 or 2 sets.

1

2

FOR: Arms, shoulders, chest (pectorals or "pecs"). Excellent for upper body, neck, arms; women's bust lines.

I suggest you first do one complete set of these exercises with lighter dumbbells (3 to 5 pounds) and a second set with heavier ones (8 to 10 pounds). Each of these exercises is done lying on bench, feet on floor. Keep elbows locked and arms absolutely straight during all four of these. Start position is always the same: dumbbells lifted straight up from your chest.

A. *Side Fly*
   1. From start position, inhale as you slowly extend arms outward to your sides, stopping when arms are parallel to the floor.
   2. Exhale and slowly return to start position.

   Do 4 to 6 repetitions per set.

B. *Circle*
   1. From start position, inhale and extend arms behind head. Keep arms straight.
   2. Slowly move arms out to the sides. Keep elbows locked.

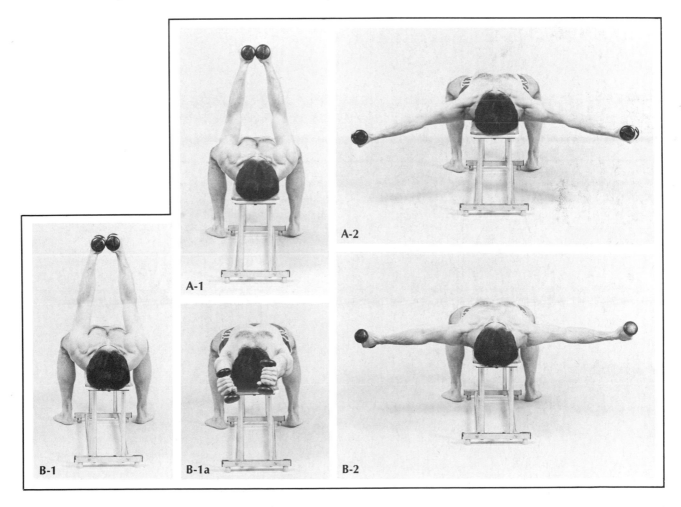

A-1

A-2

B-1

B-1a

B-2

(Continued on next page)   **135**

STRAIGHT ARM FLY ROUTINE

Weight
Training

3. Exhale as arms move toward knees and then back up to start position. Keep arms straight.

C. *Reverse Circle*

1. Same exercise as B, but reversed. From start position, inhale and slowly extend dumbbells toward your knees, bring them out and around to your sides, continue circling back toward your head, so locked elbows are by your ears.

2. Hold for a moment, then exhale and return to start position.

Do 4 to 6 circles per set.

D. *V*

1. From start position, extend arms out over your head and slightly out to the sides to form a V.

2. Bring weights back slowly to start position.

Do 6 V's per set.

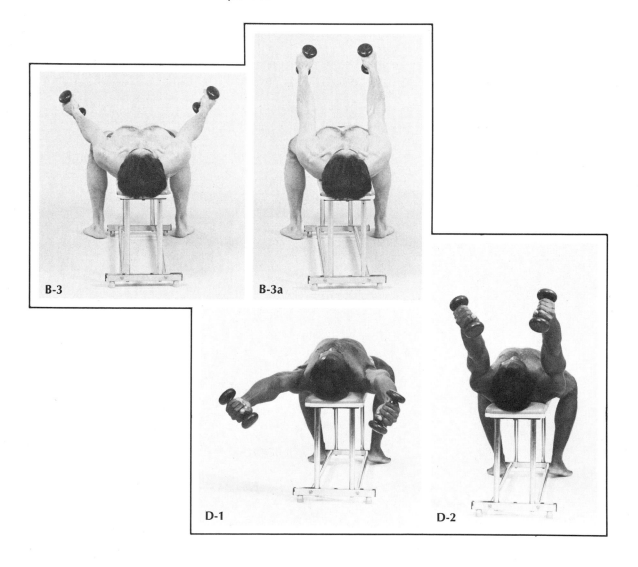

B-3

B-3a

D-1

D-2

For: Neck, tops of shoulders, backs of upper arms (triceps), inner pectorals (deltoids), bust line.

For: Neck, tops of shoulders, backs of upper arms (triceps), inner pectorals (deltoids), bust line.

STRAIGHT ARM CROSSING FLY

Weight
Training

Use a bench and a pair of small weights of not more than 5 pounds. Later, you will graduate to heavier weights.

1. Lie on bench, feet on floor, dumbbells at arm's length above chest, elbows locked. Inhale and extend arms out to the sides.
2. Bring the dumbbells together above chest but *continue* and *cross* left dumbbell over right. Hold for a moment.
3. Then repeat, move out to the sides again. Cross back again, this time right dumbbell over left.

Do 10 to 12 repetitions.

NOTE: **Do this exercise slowly for maximum benefit.**

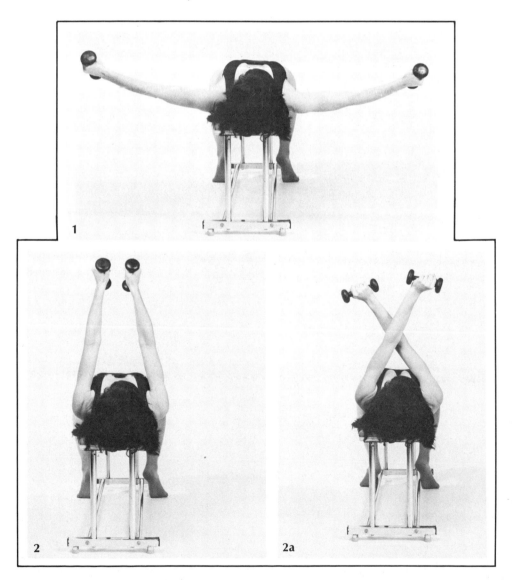

137

TIN CAN WORKOUT

Weight Training

FOR: Upper and lower back, abdomen, hips, waist, shoulders, arms, and especially the chest.

Use two cans that weigh the same, at least 10 to 14 ounces.

Starting position—hold one can in each hand. Bend over from the hip, keeping your knees locked and your chest parallel to the floor.

A. *Washboard*
   1. Extend your arms straight down toward the floor.
   2. Then bring arms up to shoulder height, bending elbows as much as possible. Keep elbows up and higher than the torso.

   Do 6 to 8 repetitions.

B. *Out–In*
   1. Extend your arms straight out in front of you, with elbows locked, parallel to the floor.
   2. Then swing back to bent elbow position.

   Do 6 to 8 repetitions.

C. *Alternate Arm Swing*
   1. Swing one arm forward and one back simultaneously.

   Do 6 to 8 repetitions.

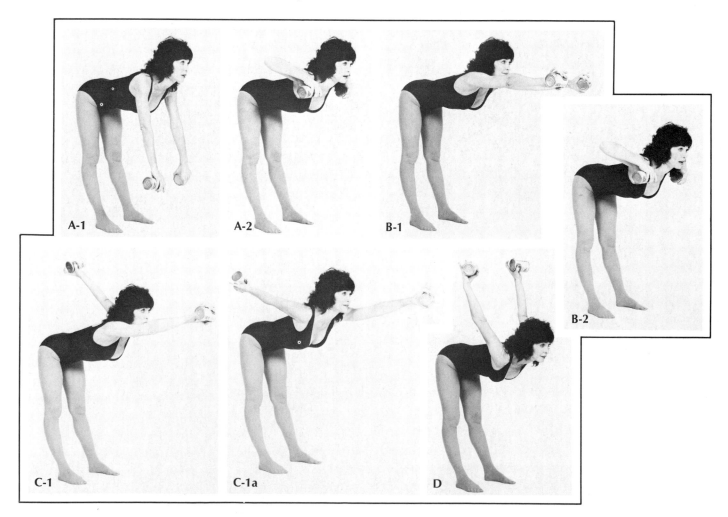

D. *Wings*
1. From starting position, lift both arms as high as you can up behind your back.

Do 6 to 8 repetitions.

E. *Cross Cans*
1. Cross your arms in front of you.
2. Then swing arms out to the sides, up as high as possible. Cross back with the other arm on top.

Do 6 to 8 repetitions.

F. *Side Stretch*
1. With both arms extended over your head, bend to one side and cross one arm over the other. Then bend to the other side doing the same thing.

Do 6 to 8 repetitions.

G. *Circle*
1. With arms directly out to the sides, keeping elbows locked, move arms in a circular motion.

Do 6 circles in one direction, then 6 circles in the other direction.

Do the seven exercises without stopping, if possible. Beginners should do the first three, then rest *briefly;* do two more, rest; then complete the remaining two. Work up gradually to doing the entire seven without stopping.

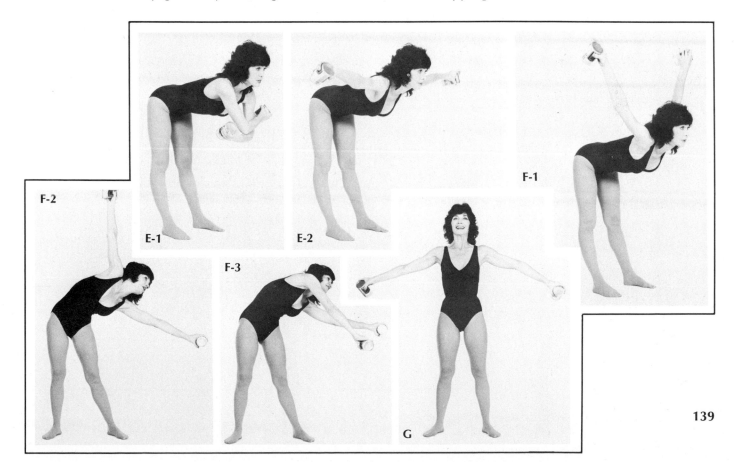

E-1   E-2   F-1

F-2   F-3   G

CLEAN AND PRESS

Weight
Training

FOR: Entire body—to perform it properly you use virtually every muscle. Enhances strength, endurance and coordination. Develops discipline, perseverance and self-confidence.

In my view, the clean and press lift is the *basic weight training exercise* and the best all-around body conditioner. It is necessary to master this particular form, as it is an essential in performing many other lifts. In addition, the principles of the clean and press should be applied when lifting anything— groceries, a child, luggage or the neighbor's piano!

Start with a bare bar, then as you master the form, add just the collars, then add to that a 1- to 2½-pound disk on each end of the bar. Then add two 5-pound disks. Then 10-pound disks, etc.

1. Stand with feet flat on floor and comfortably apart. This is the foundation for the lift. *Bend knees* and lean over with back straight, arms extended outward until you are able to grasp bar. Hands should be spaced evenly on bar slightly wider than shoulder width.

2. Using legs—*particularly buttocks and thighs*—rather than back, begin lifting straight up, keeping bar parallel to floor. As the barbell clears your knee area, start bending elbows. During clean, be sure to keep barbell moving in a straight up and down line, neither circling out and away from your body (puts strain on your back) nor coming too close and bumping it.

3. As weight passes your waist, rotate bar with your hands so your palms are facing forward. By now, legs are almost straight.

4. As the bar reaches shoulder level, knees are fully straight. Barbell is supported by your palms, firmly grasped fingers and bent elbows, which should be pointing down toward the floor. *Pause*. This is a completed clean.

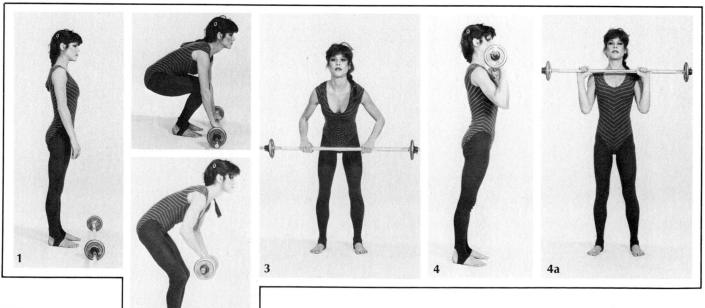

1   2   3   4   4a

5. *Inhale*—a quick short breath (this supports the press)—and lift bar smoothly straight up past chin and nose directly over your head, arms extended until elbows are locked. It is very important to keep back straight, buttocks tight, knees locked and entire body aligned throughout the press. *Pause.* This is a completed press.

6. Slowly bring barbell down in front of your face to shoulder level (clean position), *exhaling as you do. Pause.*

7. With hands tightly clasping bar, in one smooth motion, turn hands over and bend knees and guide the barbell *straight* downward using same form as you did lifting.

8. After each lift, do the Good-Morning Stretch.

Start with 6 repetitions of clean and press (bare bar or bar and collars). As you add weight, decrease number of repetitions. Do 4 to 5 or 3 to 4 repetitions as weight gets heavier. When you have reached your maximum capability in the amount of weight you are lifting, 1 to 2 clean and presses would be appropriate.

NOTES:

1. Avoid putting stress on the lower back. Lift with *legs and buttocks.* Most of the lifting should be done by the lower body, particularly the buttocks and quadriceps (thighs), with the arms acting as guides for the weight on its way up. Lifting in this manner prevents injury.

2. Another important factor when lifting is proper breathing, especially with heavier weights. Appropriately timed breathing greatly supports every lift.

3. *Avoid* letting barbell go out and away from your body.

4. *Avoid* letting barbells bump your body (especially your knees).

5. The clean and press should be done in one *smooth continuous* move except for three specific pauses. *Clean* weight from floor to shoulder level. *Pause,* take in a quick breath, then *press* weight overhead. *Pause,* then lower bar, exhaling, to shoulder level. *Pause,* then lower bar to the floor.

STRAIGHT ARM TRICEP

Weight
Training

FOR: Backs of arms (triceps). Sure cure for back-of-the-arm flabbiness.

Use a bare bar to begin with, increasing amount of weight as you progress.

1. Clean and press bar over your head, holding the bar with hands *closer together* than in the usual clean and press.

2. Making sure your upper arms from armpit to elbow remain stationary and close to your ears, *inhale slowly,* bend your elbows, lowering bar down behind you as far as you are able. Hold for a second.

3. Then exhale and bring bar back up to overhead press position.

Do 6 to 8 repetitions.

FOR: Increased definition in the shoulders and back.

1. Place barbell with appropriate weight for you directly in front of you; feet far enough apart so you can reach the bar keeping your back level.

2. Bending from the hips, keeping knees locked, grasp bar and lift from the floor with straight arms. Raise your torso until your chest is parallel to the floor.

3. Bending your arms, bring bar up and in toward your chest. Continue in a circular motion past your neck and chin, then out and down toward the floor again as if you were "rowing a boat."

Do 6 to 8 repetitions.

NOTES:
1. **Don't jerk the bar up—fluid motion up and around and down.**
2. **Be careful not to hit your chin on circular motion before coming down.**
3. **Don't let bar touch floor after each rep—you don't want to break the rhythm.**

BEHIND NECK PRESS (Seated)

Weight Training

FOR: Trapeziuses ("traps"), neck and shoulder muscles, arms and upper back.

Place amount of weight on bar that is appropriate for you.

1. Stand a few inches in front of bench.
2. Clean and press barbell, lowering it to behind the neck position.
3. Carefully back up until you are straddling the bench. Sit down, back straight, feet firmly on floor.
4. Inhale and press weight straight up, keeping bar in back of head until arms are fully extended with elbows locked.
5. Then exhale and lower bar to behind neck position. Be careful not to bump your head with bar.

Do 6 to 8 repetitions in each set—up to 3 sets.

NOTE: **Increase amount of weight or number of sets as your strength develops.**

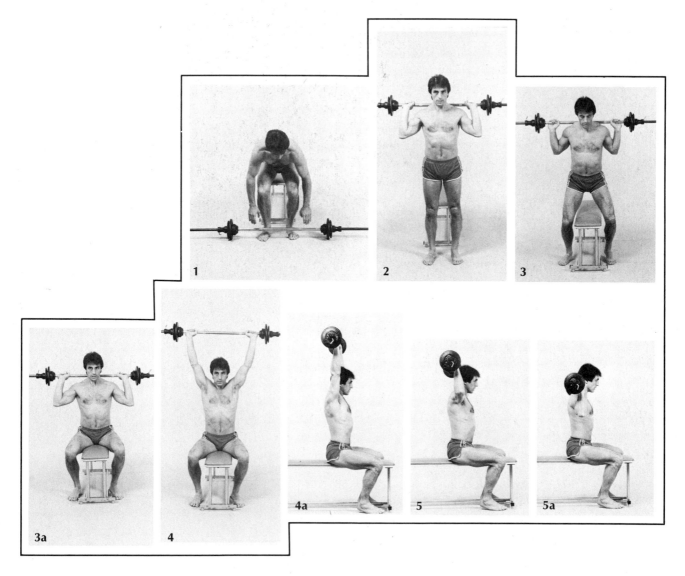

FOR: Trapeziuses, neck and shoulder muscles, arms and upper back.

Place amount of weight on bar that is appropriate for you.

1. Legs comfortably spaced, knees locked, back straight, feet firmly on the floor.
2. Clean and press barbell. When lowering bar, place it behind the neck.
3. *Inhale* and press weight straight up, keeping bar in back of head until arms are fully extended with elbows locked.
4. Then exhale and lower bar to behind neck position. Be careful not to bump your head with bar.

Do 6 to 8 repetitions in each set—up to 3 sets.

NOTES:
1. **Increase amount of weight or number of sets as your strength develops.**
2. **In standing positions, the tendency is to use the lower body and legs to assist in lift. Avoid this (use neck, shoulders, arms, upper back) because this exercise is designed for the upper body.**

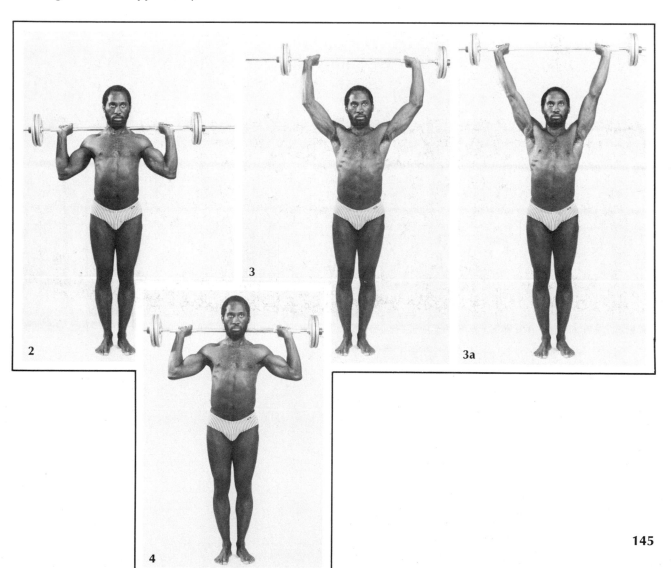

FRONT SQUAT
(Standing Flat)

Weight
Training

FOR: Buttocks, fronts of thighs.

Use a bare bar at first to get the "feel" of this exercise. Then add weight as your strength and confidence increases.

1. Clean bar up to chest-high position.
2. With feet comfortably apart, inhale and slowly bend knees (keep your back as straight as possible, and heels on the floor) to a point about halfway down to the floor.
3. Exhale and slowly rise back up out of squat, straightening knees to come to standing position with knees locked.
4. Repeat process, but this time go down three-quarters of the way. Inhale going down. Exhale coming up.
5. On your third squat, go all the way down to where your knees are as bent as they can be. Keep back straight.

After doing half and three-quarter squats, do 6 to 8 full squats.

NOTES:
1. **Don't let knees at any time go wider than they are at the start of the exercise.**
2. **Try to create a rhythm with the exercise in going down and coming up.**
3. **Take a deep breath on descent and exhale on the ascent.**
4. **From all the squats, particularly the deepest one, use buttocks and thighs to rise up to standing position.**

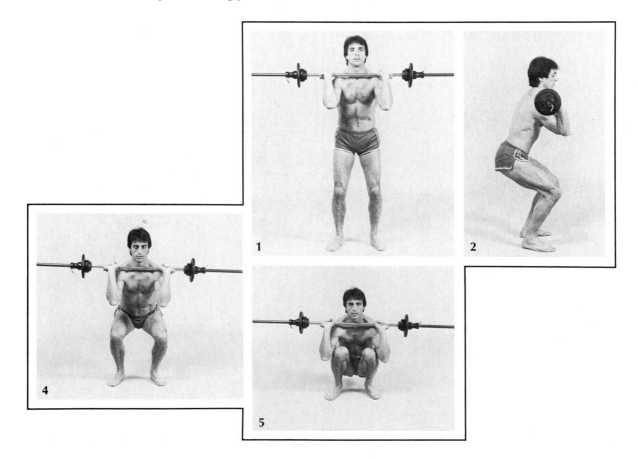

FOR: Buttocks, fronts of thighs, with additional benefit for calves (because heels are elevated).

Use appropriate amount of weight. Place phone book on the floor just behind you.

1. Clean bar up to chest position.

2. Step back carefully, placing your heels up on the phone book while your toes remain on the floor.

3. As in the Front Squat, inhale and slowly bend knees to a point about halfway down to the floor.

4. Exhale and slowly rise back up out of squat, straightening knees to come to standing position with knees locked.

5. Repeat process, but this time go down three-quarters of the way. Inhale going down. Exhale going up.

6. On the third squat, go all the way down to where your knees are as bent as they can be. Keep back straight.

7. From all squats, particularly the deepest one, use buttocks and thighs to rise up to the standing positions.

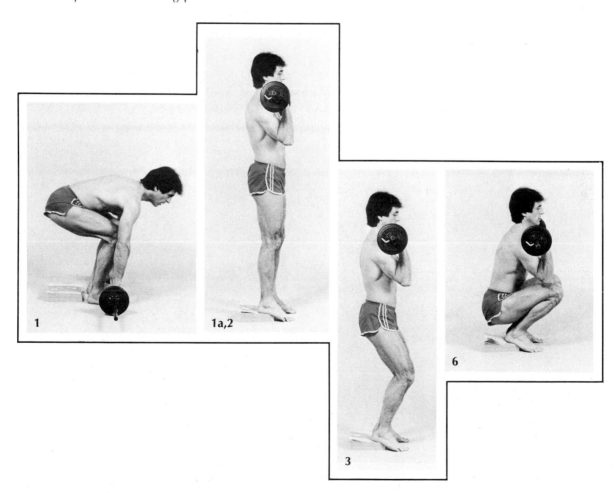

BEHIND NECK SQUAT
(Standing Flat)

Weight
Training

FOR: Buttocks, backs of thighs, calves.

Use amount of weight appropriate for you, with the goal of increasing it as you get stronger.

1. Clean and press bar up over your head.

2. Bend elbows and slowly lower bar behind your head onto your shoulders, keeping it balanced across back of neck.

3. When bar is in place, *inhale* and begin to squat by slowly bending your knees. Continue downward, heels on the floor, back as straight as possible. (Even though you need to lean out and forward slightly for balance, don't let your back collapse over.)

4. As with front squats, continue in one slow, steady move—halfway to floor, then come up the same way. Then squat three-quarters of the way down and return to standing position. By now you are warmed up and can go down as far as possible. Your goal is to be in a full squat, with your knèes bent as far as they are able. Work to come up as controlled and steady as you descend.

After 2 initial warm-ups (halfway down and three-quarters of the way), do 6 to 8 full squats.

NOTES:
1. **Stay with the same rhythm going down and coming up; don't let the weight fall down or jerk the weight up, but go down smoothly and come up smoothly.**
2. **Stay within same form, especially not allowing your knees to go out to the side. I usually say, "Don't let your knees go off to the Joneses'."**
3. ***Inhale going down** and **exhale coming up.***

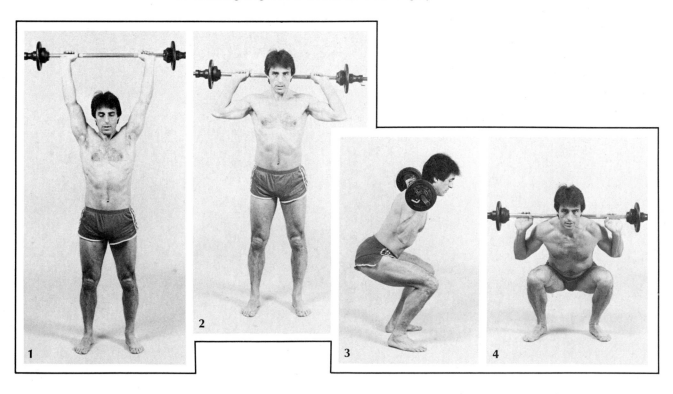

1   2   3   4

FOR: Buttocks, backs of thighs, calves, hamstrings.

Use appropriate amount of weight. Place phone book on the floor just in back of where you will lift bar.

1. Clean and press bar up over head.
2. Bend elbows and slowly lower bar behind your head onto your shoulders keeping it balanced across back of neck.
3. Step back carefully, placing your heels up on the phone book while toes remain on the floor. Do the same exercise as Behind Neck Squat except with your heels on the phone book.

Do 6 to 8 repetitions after 2 initial warm-ups.

NOTE: **Keep heels firmly on phone book throughout exercise.**

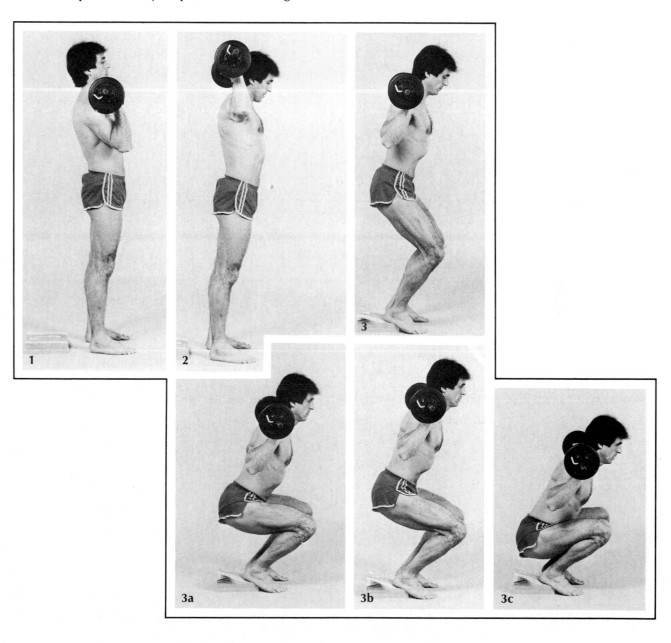

STRAIGHT ARM PULLOVER

Weight
Training

FOR: Arms, shoulders (deltoids), chest, entire torso—including abdomen, upper back, shoulder blades, and Rimboid area (immediately below the shoulder blades in your back). Counteracts "round shoulders" and assists total body alignment.

Start out using just a bare bar, then add just the collars, then later 2½ pounds on each side, then 5 pounds on each side, and on up—whatever weight that is appropriate for your level of training.

1. Lie down with your head right at the end of the bench and your feet placed firmly on the floor.
2. Lift barbell straight up from your chest until arms are fully extended, elbows locked.
3. *Inhale* and with your arms absolutely straight, slowly move bar directly back over face and head until arms are outstretched beside your head and are parallel to the floor. Be careful not to allow the bar to drop below bench level. Pause for a moment.
4. Exhale as you bring bar slowly back up to start position.

Do 8 to 10 repetitions.

NOTE: **Use your upper back, chest and arms to lift weight. *Do not* use your lower back.**

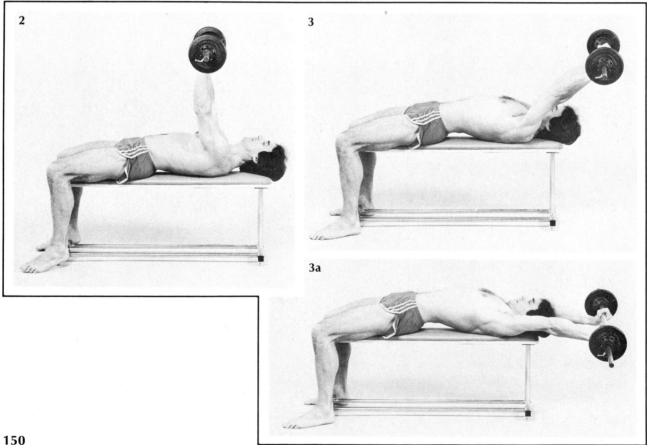

FOR: Pectorals ("pecs"), chest (bust line), rib cage, upper back, shoulders, arms (triceps, biceps), forearms and wrists. Tightens abdomen.

Place appropriate weight disks on bar. Elevate one end of bench on two or three phone books. Place these carefully, making sure bench is secure. This is so your arms will not reach the floor as you do this exercise. The longer your arms, the more you will need to elevate the bench.

1. Clean (one clean motion lifting weight up to shoulders) the bar to chest height.
2. Carefully straddle bench and sit with your head toward the elevated end.
3. Controlling the weight (still in clean position) slowly roll down onto your back. Your shoulders should be firmly on bench, feet and toes on the floor for balance, your head just off the end of bench.

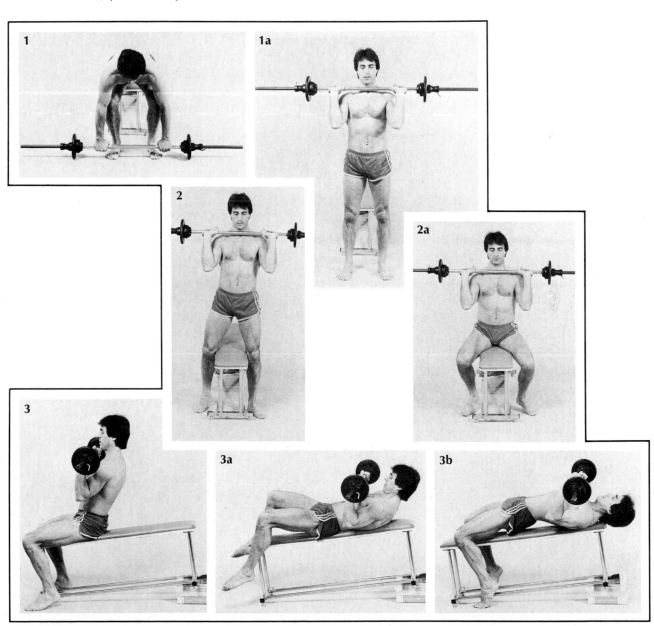

(Continued on next page)

BENT ARM PULLOVER

Weight
Training

4. Inhale and lift bar, with elbows bent, up from chest (4 to 8 inches), crossing over face and head in a slow circular motion.

5. Continue controlling the bar back and down toward the floor as far as you can; body arched up off bench. Keep control of yourself and the weight by using buttocks and thighs to stay centered on bench.

6. Hold for a moment in extended position.

7. Then, slowly bring the bar back up in the same form in which you lowered it. (*Exhale* on return). Continue up, around, over face and back to start position at chest.

Do 6 repetitions per set.

NOTES:

1. **If you are new to weight training, start light and gradually increase amount of weight as you determine what you can handle, but not so light that you don't get a workout. Remember, the idea is to tax yourself *without injury*.**

2. **Don't break the rhythm. Keep every rep very fluid going down and back.**

3. **Be constantly aware of a strong (or tight) grip on the bar so it won't slip or accidentally hit any part of your body.**

4. **Your breathing will help you perform this exercise more beneficially.**

14

CARDIOVASCULAR ACTIVITIES and WARM-UPS

For general fitness and conditioning, endurance, stamina, enhancing the circulatory system—for all ages.

Though running is my favorite cardiovascular exercise, and I believe it is the most beneficial of all, others prefer bicycling, rowing, jogging, fast walking. Whatever the preference, the idea is to tax the body's heart/blood system. Nevertheless, caution must be used in entering any of these activities. The beginner, especially, must be made aware of his or her limitations. Pain is seldom gain, and trying to do too much too soon—to run, bike, swim or row too far—is simply self-defeating and possibly dangerous. Each type of exercise works different parts of the body. Running and biking are of the greatest benefit to the lower body. Jogging, the slow way to run, and fast walking have somewhat the same benefits. All four methods of exercise greatly enhance the circulatory system. The total and champion cardiovascular conditioner is swimming, for it demands using far more of the muscle structure and helps to increase circulation throughout the body. But not everyone cares that much about swimming, and not everyone has access to a pool on a regular basis. While I recommend swimming to everyone, I usually start my clients on walking/jogging routines. Space in which to walk or jog is usually available to everyone.

1st two weeks   Begin with 5 minutes of stretch exercises. Walk at least 30 minutes daily, slowly increasing stride and speed each day. End with 5 minutes of stretch exercises.

CARDIOVASCULAR ACTIVITIES

153

2nd two weeks	Begin with 5 minutes of stretch exercises. Walk for 5 minutes; slowly jog for 30 seconds; alternate the brisk walking and jogging 6 times. Stretch exercises.
3rd two weeks	Begin with 5 minutes of stretch exercises. Walk for 5 minutes; jog for 1 minute; alternate 5 times. Stretch exercises.
4th two weeks	Begin with 5 minutes of stretch exercises. Walk for 4 minutes; slowly jog for 2 minutes; alternate 5 times. Stretch exercises.
5th two weeks	Begin with 5 minutes of stretch exercises. Walk for 3 minutes; slowly jog for 2 minutes. Alternate 6 times. Stretch exercises.
6th two weeks	Begin with 5 minutes of stretch exercises. Walk briskly for 2 minutes; speed up jogging for 2 minutes. Alternate 7 times. Stretch exercises.
7th two weeks	Begin with 5 minutes of stretch exercises. Walk briskly for 1 minute; jog for 3 minutes. Alternate 7 times. Stretch exercises.
8th two weeks	Begin with 5 minutes of stretch exercises. Walk briskly 1 minute; jog for 4 minutes. Alternate 5 times. Stretch exercises.

At this point, you should be able to shift over into the jogging routine, but jog slowly, gradually adding speed as the days go by.

I know runners who believe they must pound the pavement an hour a day. For myself and most other people, a half hour is plenty. The same applies to biking, swimming, rowing or any other form of cardiovascular exercise.

WHEN? I think that 4 days a week is enough. I run Tuesday, Thursday, Saturday and Sunday. By mixing weight lifting and stretching routines on the other days, boredom is fended off. Mornings are best for me.

TIPS 1. Warm up with nice, easy runner's stretches, which also work for bikers, swimmers, rowers, rope jumpers, fast walkers. Always be gentle with your body during these stretches.

2. Everyone's body is different, everyone's "night before" is different, but I always begin running very slowly, continuing the warm-up from the stretches. I may go for 5 minutes before shifting into higher gear, lengthening stride. Some people prefer 10 minutes at slow speed. There are no rules here. Take your time. You may be sore from the day before; maybe you're not in the mood. Be comfortable and enjoy the run, jog or fast walk.

3. Again, everyone's body is different but I would avoid doing any of the cardiovascular exercises on a full stomach. I prefer to run on an empty or near-empty stomach.

4. Young or old, avoid high heat. Do these exercises in the cool of the morning or evening—except swimming, of course. Aquatic exercises have a built-in coolant.

5. Avoid doing cardiovascular exercises in areas where there is heavy air pollution.

6. In extremely cold weather, dress warmly. In near-zero weather, put a scarf over your mouth to filter out the icy air.

7. A "cooling off" period after cardiovascular exercises is extremely important. You should not just *stop* after a half hour of vigorous exercising. You must slow down the heart, the body. I walk for about 5 minutes during this period. A rower or biker should slow the pace way down for a similar or longer period.

8. Bikers and rowers should also do a series of post-exercise stretches. They've been hunched over at least 30 minutes and should stretch the upper body muscles and the leg and thigh muscles.

Whoever first said, "Run for your life"—maybe a caveman—was exactly right.

OVERALL STRETCH AND RELAXER

Cardiovascular Stretch

FOR: Stretches upper and lower body, creates an overall feeling of relaxation, alleviates stress, stabilizes breathing.

Use any waist-high, stationary object that you can grasp hold of.

1. With feet slightly apart and elbows locked, grasp the support and descend slowly.

2. Bend knees and lean back as you proceed, moving down the support.

3. When you reach a full squat, *inhale* deeply, distending midsection. Feel that the entire circumference of your waist (back included) moves outward to the fullest extent. Hold breath 3 counts, exhale for 3 counts. Do 3 reps.

4. After completing Step 3, release head downward, letting chin touch chest, totally relaxed. Lean back and feel the tension released.

5. Hold for 10 seconds and then slowly bring your head upright and start slowly up the support, your thighs supporting your ascent. Keep back straight and aligned. Return to start position.

Do this exercise as many times during the day as you wish.

NOTES:
1. **This exercise is perfect for "catching your breath" after a cardiovascular exercise such as running, biking, swimming, etc.**
2. **This exercise also provides a feeling of total relaxation after a stressful situation or anytime during the day.**

FOR: Before jogging or running, or even fast walking, give your body a break and do three simple stretches.

1. Sitting, spread your legs as if actually running, or hurdling. Stretch the calf, thigh and groin muscles. This is not a "touching" exercise (though you touch both feet); it is a pulling exercise.

2. Spread your legs and again touch both feet, which should be in a V position. Feel the groin stretch, as well as your lower back, and knees.

3. With the legs in a modified lotus, hands clasping toes, stretch the upper body forward and let the legs resist. This is a simultaneous flexibility stretch for the groin, thighs, lower back, lower and upper abdomen.

NOTES: **Each position should be held at least 5 to 10 seconds. No jarring or bouncing. Ease into stretch releasing muscles slowly.**

ASSORTED STRETCHES

Pre- and
Post-Cardiovascular

FOR: Complete stretch of the legs before and after running, biking, etc.

1. Feet crossed, lean over and touch the ground. Switch legs and repeat. Do *not* bounce.

2. With hands flat against tree, wall, etc., rise on one foot (other foot crossed at ankle) lean forward. Switch legs.

3. Standing on one leg, bend other leg behind you and grasp it with opposite arm. Switch legs.

4. Sitting on ground, one leg stretched in front of you and the other bent to the side, *slowly* lean back until you are lying on the ground. Do *not* overextend yourself. Switch legs.

Do each stretch until you feel stretched out enough to run, walk, bike easily.

FOR: Before running.

1. Start position: hands clasped behind back, body bent over; feet flat on ground.

2. Flex left knee forward, hold 10 seconds. Return to start position.

3. Flex right knee forward, hold 10 seconds. Return to start position.

Do 5 repetitions.

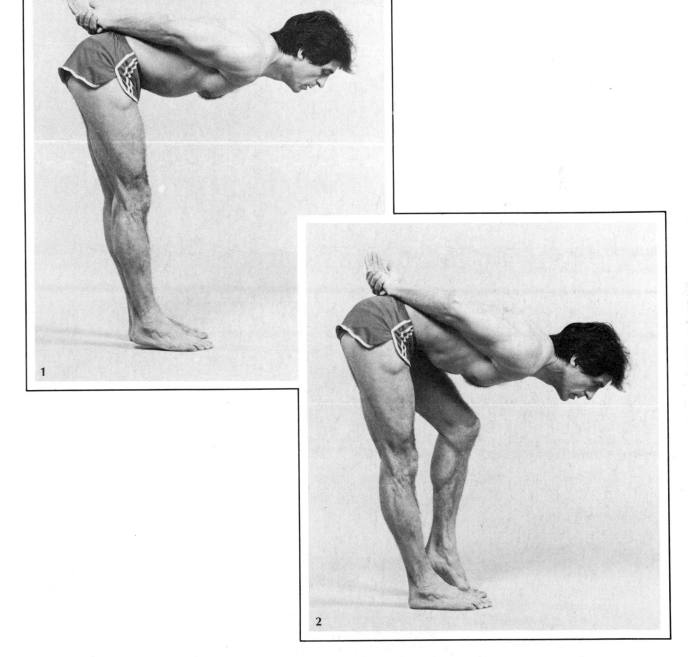

LOOSENING STRETCHES

Pre-Cardiovascular

FOR: Stretching before and after running.

1. *Torso Twist*
   Arms extended above head. Twist to each side.
   Do 10 repetitions.

2. *Bicycle*
   Using arms as support, lie on back and begin the bicycle motion.
   Do for 1 to 3 minutes.

3. *Knee Lift*
   Raise each knee to chest.
   Do 10 repetitions, alternating.

NOTE: **Build up repetitions or time as you become more advanced.**

One of the best heart exercises is steady walking up and down steps (instead of taking escalators and elevators!). Slowly extend yourself going up and down for 20 to 30 seconds. Rest for a minute. Resume for another 20 to 30 seconds.

Do 3 or 4 sets with a minute's rest in between.

NOTE: Keep in mind your current state of health. Don't overtax or overextend yourself suddenly. Gradually extend yourself with caution and awareness of how your body is responding.

1

SQUAT JUMPS

Cardiovascular

FOR: To do in rainy weather; gets your heart pumping and oxygen flowing.

1. Start in a squat position with heels off the floor. Hands are on hips or extended in front.
2. Leap as high in the air as you can, coming down on the balls of your feet.
3. *Control* the landing.

Do 8 to 10 repetitions rapidly.

Then, *jump in place,* going 6 to 8 inches off the floor, about 20 times.

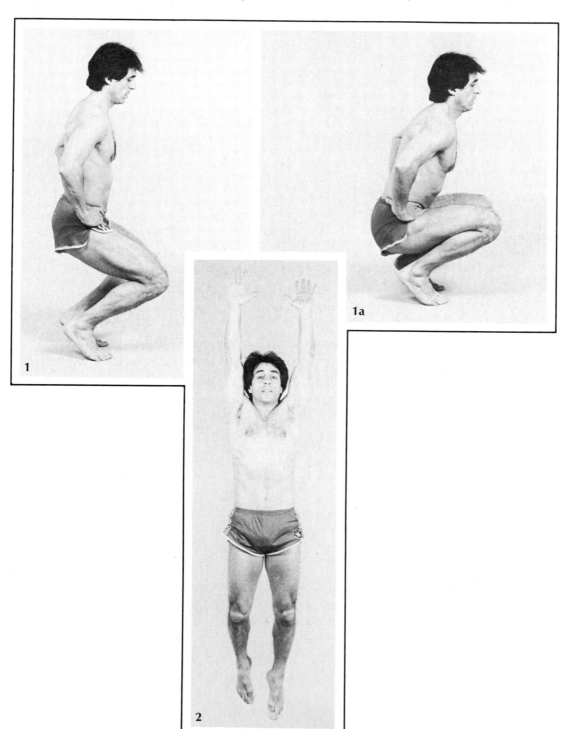

15

PARTNERS

For physical fitness togetherness, working out with a partner is not only fun, but offers some advantages in muscle resistance. Time passes quicker, with laughs and fun. Partnering is for any age, and definitely unisex.

I try very hard to sell fitness and wellness to all people of all ages—singles, married couples, families, extended families, retirees in all assortments. There's a contagion I've seen at work in group exercising—whole floors thudding with bodies—that is also catchable at home. Girlfriend gets bit by it and infects boyfriend. Husband infects wife, children. Male Gray Panther infects female Gray Panther. *If exercising alone bores you, find a partner.*

WHEN? Any time when both partners are available—morning, noon or night.

HOW? See exercises beginning on next page.

TIPS 1. If there is a size and weight difference between you and your partner, compensate on every exercise to narrow that difference. There is a tendency, usually not on purpose, to "push" the partner; to "over-power." When that happens, both partners lose.

2. In addition to fun and togetherness, work toward feeling muscle

resistance in all these exercises; feel the "tug o' war" between the muscles.

3. Don't limit yourself to my examples in this book. Experiment and find new ways to exercise together.

4. Music, I've found, adds a lot to partner conditioning. The nature of the "seesaw" exercises alone is rhythmical.

If two heads are often better than one, four arms and legs are often better than two.

FOR: Upper body.

Partners exert equal resistance, palm against palm, in a circular movement up above the head, out to the sides and back to the starting position in one smooth continuous motion.

Do 8 repetitions slowly.

DOUBLE SQUAT

Partners

FOR: Posture, release of back, vertebrae stretch (especially the lower back), leg and thigh area.

1. Standing opposite your partner, clasp hands. *Very slowly* bend knees, leaning back slightly—just enough to support each other's body weight.

2. Slowly descend—pausing along the way of your descent if you wish—until finally you are both in a squat with arms extended and elbows locked.

3. Lean back and *slowly* drop head forward and *totally release* entire back and shoulder area. Do not let go of partner's hands in this position.

4. Inhale slowly until you fill entire waistline and lower back with air—like a bellows. Hold, then exhale *slowly* and completely.

5. Lift head upright and come up as slowly as you descended, stopping at different levels to add additional resistance to entire area below the waist.

Do 2 or 3 repetitions.

NOTE: **Stay level with your partner—descend and ascend at the same rate of speed *slowly!* You can naturally compensate for disparate size and strength—every few inches stop for a moment (count of 5) then continue descent.**

FOR: Arms, shoulders and neck, backs of arms.

1. Hold towel overhead with arms extended; partner grasps rolled towel behind your neck.
2. Partner begins to pull on towel while you pull against it.
3. Continue pulling until your forearms are parallel with floor.

Do 8 to 10 repetitions, build up to 20 and then switch places.

VARIATION:

1. Lie down on stomach with elbows bent. Keep elbows on floor throughout exercise.
2. Partner kneels above you pulling towel up as you resist. You pull towel toward floor.

Do 8 to 10 repetitions, build up to 20 and then switch places.

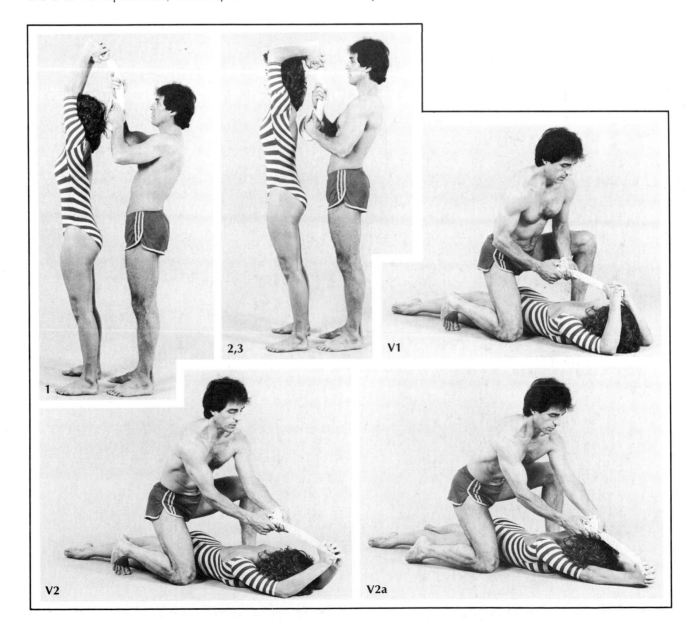

1   2,3   V1   V2   V2a

ONE-ARM PUSH AND RESIST

Partners

FOR: Arms and shoulders.

1. Sit with your legs over your partner's; opposite palm to partner's.
2. As one partner pushes slowly, the other resists and vice versa. Person who is pushing breathes in while person resisting exhales.

Do 10 repetitions on each arm.

FOR: Entire upper torso, including arm and shoulder area.

Grasping partner's arm at the wrist, with one arm behind your back, pull backward as far as possible while partner resists and vice versa.

Do 10 repetitions on each arm.

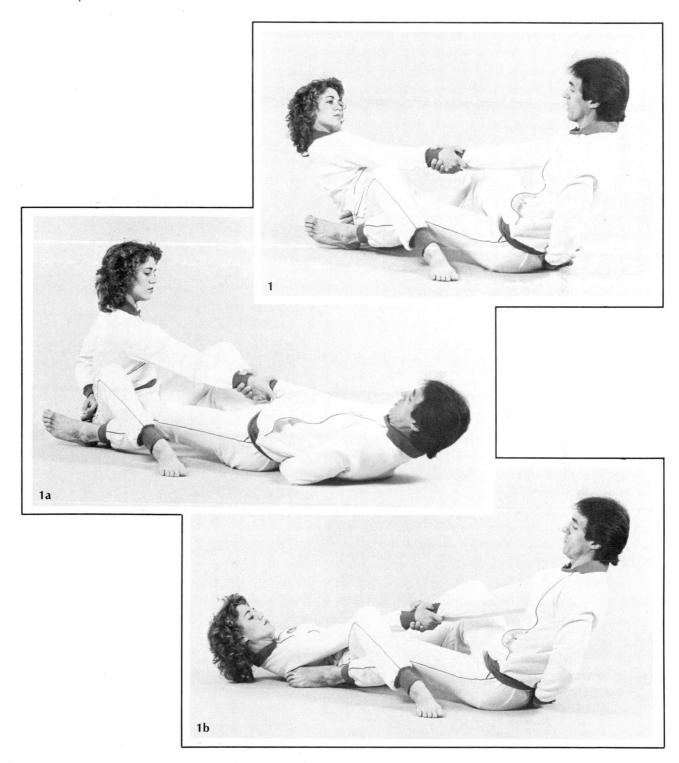

PULL AND STRETCH
(SeeSaw Stretch)

Partners

FOR: Upper torso, shoulders, lower back, abdominals.

1. Sit on floor facing each other; clasp wrists. One partner's legs over and on the outside of the other.

2. *Slowly* allow one partner to lie back so the body is stretched out on the floor.

3. Then reverse the process.

Do 10 repetitions—5 in each direction.

NOTE: **As with all pull and resist or push and resist exercises, partners should give according to the other person's strength and/or weakness.**

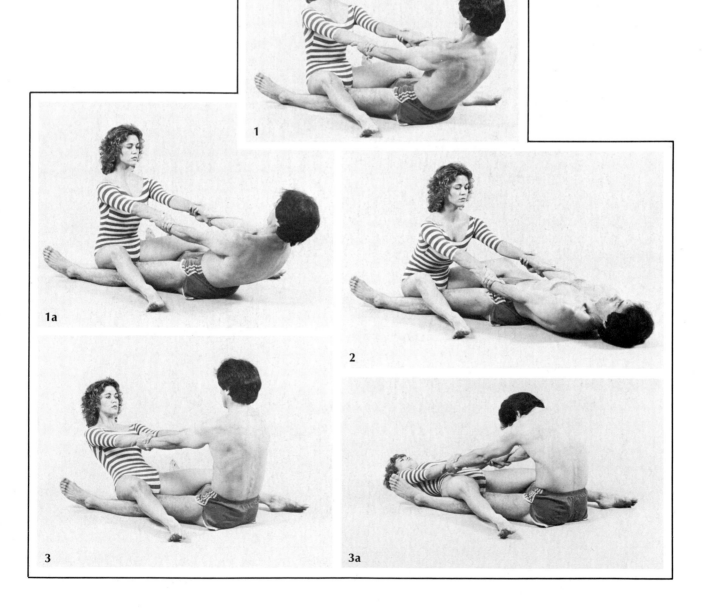

FOR: Back, shoulder, neck and head area.

1. Sit on floor facing partner. One partner's legs are on the outside and one on the inside. Hands are clasped behind each other's necks.

2. One partner pulls back and away as far as possible without breaking the mutual neck clasp. Slowly reverse the process.

Do 10 repetitions in each direction.

NOTE: **Pull** *slowly*—**don't jerk partner's head and neck area.**

ONE-FOOT PUSH AND RESIST

Partners

FOR: Toning and stretching legs, thighs, groin, buttocks and abdomen.

1. Lie on floor with one person's legs within the partner's legs, far enough away for maximum stretch.

2. Push against the partner's opposite foot, alternating legs. Pressure should be felt throughout entire lower body.

Do 10 repetitions with each foot for each person.

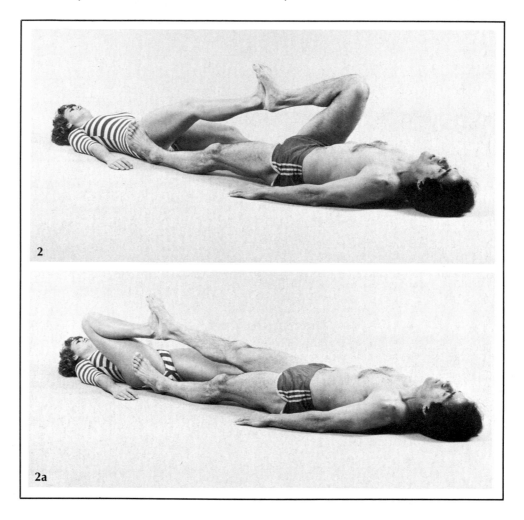

For: Legs, thighs, groin, buttocks, abdomen.

1. Lying on back, with knees bent, put soles of feet against those of partner.

2. Push back and forth, slowly, working toward maximum stretch. Keep small of the back flat against the floor.

Do 20 repetitions (10 each direction).

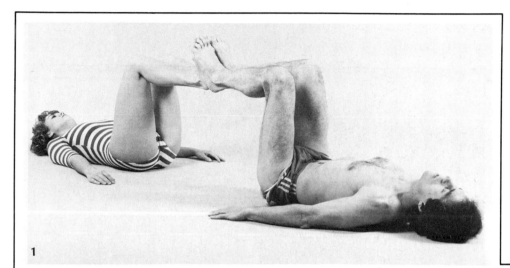

1

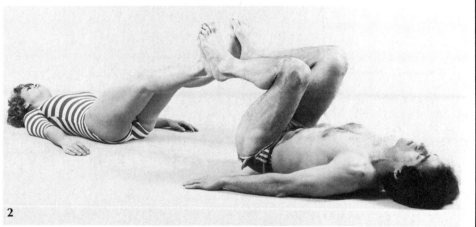

2

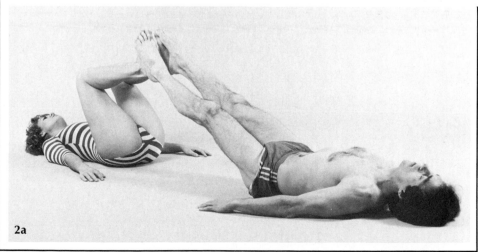

2a

DOUBLE-FOOT GROIN STRETCH

Partners

FOR: Groin, thighs, abdomen, buttocks, knees.

1. Lying on your back with knees bent, place soles of feet against partner's.

2. Keeping soles of feet against partner's at all times, straighten legs up toward ceiling. Use extended arms to anchor body.

3. Open legs as wide as possible, keeping them straight, and extend them out to the side.

4. Bend knees and slowly return to start position.

Do 3 or 4 repetitions.

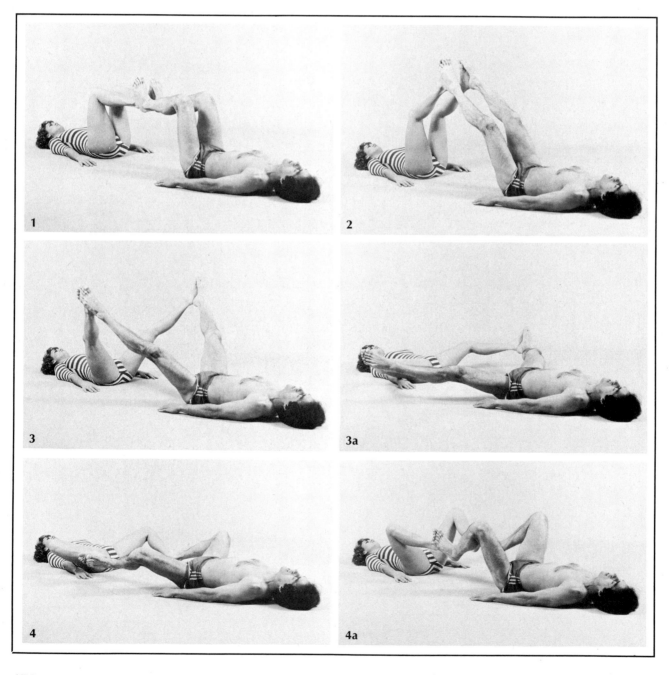

FOR: Groin, inner and outer thighs, hips, buttocks and abdomen.

1. Lying on the floor, both partners extend legs toward the ceiling with ankles touching. The "resister" is on the outside and the "pusher" is on the inside. Both *must keep knees locked* throughout exercise. The temptation to bend knees will be great.

2. Pusher starts pushing partner's legs slowly and steadily apart while resister attempts to keep legs together.

3. When resister's legs are at their maximum open position, resister pushes with a constant steady pressure to bring legs back up to start position. Pusher resists the upward movement.

4. Back at start position, partners change position of legs so original resister is now the pusher and vice versa.

NOTE: **If your partner isn't as flexible as you are, don't force him/her to a point farther than his/her body can go.**

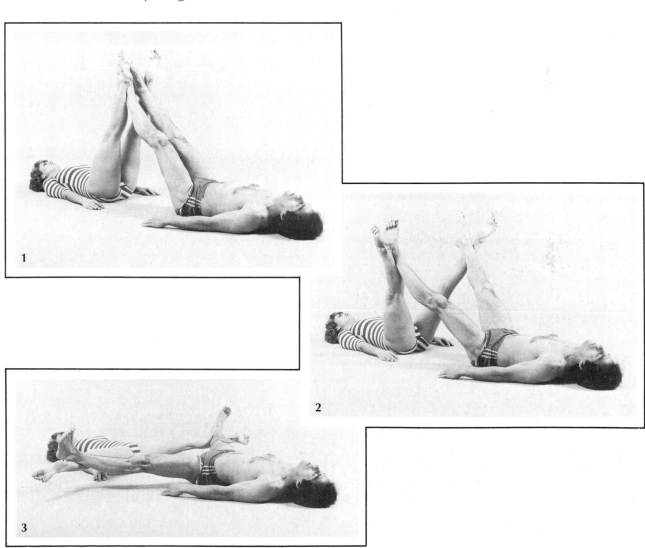

TANDEM BICYCLE

Partners

FOR: Legs, thighs, groin, buttocks, abdomen and cardiovascular system.

1. Lying on the floor, feet sole-to-sole, place bodies so that maximum muscle resistance can be achieved. Alternate pushes must be resisted by both partners.

2. Bicycle 3 to 5 minutes one way, then reverse the motion for another 3 to 5 minutes.

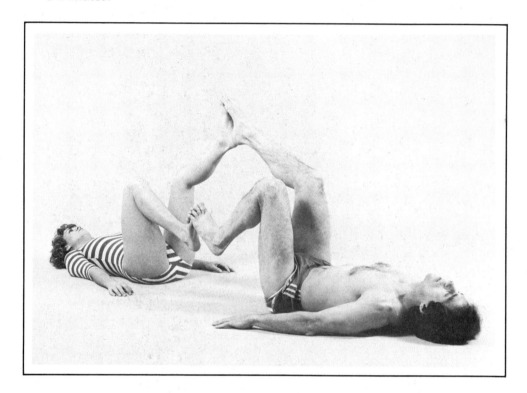

FOR: Total release of tension; relaxation for the entire body.

1. Partners begin by standing one behind the other. Partner in back is the puppeteer; partner in front is the puppet. Puppeteer places one hand on puppet's waist; the other with fingers touching topmost vertebra of spinal column.

2. Puppet slowly bends forward, keeping knees straight. With thumb, puppeteer follows vertebra along down spinal column and steadies puppet with other hand to give puppet total concentration on the feeling of disconnection of each vertebra. Once puppet is bent forward as far as possible, puppet should *not* attempt any stretching of arms.

3. Puppet remains in forward-bent position for 10 seconds, concentrating on feeling of disconnection of vertebrae, then puppet slowly reverses the process, unfolding upward, starting at the base of the spine. Puppeteer's thumb now travels up the spine, as puppet feels the reconnection of vertebrae until reaching upright position.

Switch positions and perform exercise.

NOTES:
1. **The puppet should keep knees straight at all times.**
2. **The puppeteer should help the puppet maintain balance throughout the exercise.**

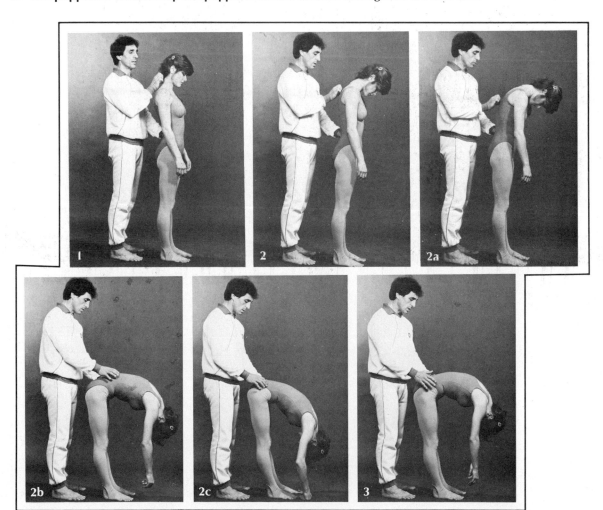

FLOATING

Partners

This is an exercise that produces the feeling of floating—no gravity; being totally suspended. This is a technique I have utilized with a great variety of clients—tiny women; 6-feet-tall, 200-pound men; young children; and even individuals over 90 years of age. It stretches out the spine in a very gentle manner. The person's own body weight elongates the spinal column, decompresses the vertebrae, alleviates tension and stress, and delivers complete, head-to-toe relaxation. In fact, after they've experienced it, people have likened the feeling to floating on a cloud. (Hence the name, which is—don't you think—better than "Client on My Back"?)

I don't feel that this exercise is practical if one partner is much taller and heavier and stronger than the other. To balance out differences in size and weight, I've found that standing on a raised level such as weights, wood, etc. helps. I don't suggest trying this exercise unless you feel adequate in handling your partner.

1. Stand back to back; arms extended overhead with elbows locked. The initiator grabs wrists of partner.

178

2. The initiator, with hold on partner's wrists, bends knees so that buttocks is placed between partner's buttocks and hamstrings.

3. The initiator lifts partner off floor.

4. The initiator leans over so that both upper bodies are parallel to the floor.

5. The initiator now releases partner's wrists and slowly reaches back with his hands to place them on partner's knees.

6. With initiator's hands holding partner's knees, the initiator slowly bends forward so that the partner's body is now arched over with head leaning toward the ground.

7. After being in this position for 10 to 30 seconds, the initiator brings his upper body parallel to the ground while bringing hands back to grab partner's wrists. Initiator slowly straightens back up.

8. Once bodies are in upright position, the initiator slowly stretches partner's arms out to the side and back down to finish with hands and arms alongside the body.

5a,6

7

7a

8

8a

16

PRE-SENIOR CITIZEN

I have placed certain unisex exercises in the "pre-senior" category with the understanding that some pre-seniors are quite capable of doing any exercise in this book. As far as I'm concerned, there are no limitations because of age. Physical condition prescribes limitations, not birthdays.

Some wise people exercise all their lives, and move into their mid-fifties in good physical condition. Unfortunately, the majority of people do not. The latter would do well to check with a physician prior to entering any type of conditioning program. Even with a physician's blessing, *go slow* is my motto. Taking on too much will only lead to pain and discouragement. Ease into the stretching, the weight lifting (start with a bare bar) and particularly with the cardiovascular exercises discussed previously.

WHEN?   Exactly when you feel like it! A pre-senior has earned the right to set the exercise program at whatever hour pleases him or her.

HOW?   Use the examples on the following pages or any other pages throughout this book.

TIPS   1. Know the physical condition of your body. Do not mentally talk yourself into believing you're in good or even fair condition, when the opposite happens to be true. Being a realist will help you, not hurt you.

2. Choose the place in which you work out with an eye toward comfort.

3. Do not work out during periods of high heat.

4. *Set your own pace.* Your workout doesn't need to be extended. In fact, finishing up exhausted defeats the purpose.

5. Pick and choose among the exercises and lifts. Only do those with which *you* feel comfortable.

Take a long, close look at the model June Tatro on the following pages. The lady is in her early seventies.

KINKS-OUT STRETCH

Pre-Senior
Citizen

FOR: Entire upper body; abdomen through torso and arms and shoulders.

Stand with legs comfortably apart. Put both arms over your head; then reach for the ceiling with one arm extended upward while bending the other. Hold extended position for a second or two. Reverse arm positions, stretching other arm.

Do 6 to 8 repetitions with each arm.

FOR: Backs, thighs, calves, midsection, buttocks.

1. Stand with feet apart and bend over from the waist as far as possible, knees locked.

2. Hold for a few seconds.

3. Then crisscross arms laterally. Reach for the floor with elbows.

4. Hold for another few seconds.

5. Then extend both hands between legs. Hold position.

6. Then do alternate toe touches.

Do whole sequence 2 or 3 times.

NOTE: Do not *bounce* in stretch position; rather, slowly go as far as you can and then just a "hair" more. This is the way to increase flexibility without injury.

183

LUNGE
STRETCH-UP

Pre-Senior
Citizen
(Stretching)

FOR: The entire body, particularly the Achilles tendon.

1. Assume lunge position—back leg as straight as possible with the heel up, leg pushing toward the floor.

2. Reach both hands up over your head, bringing hands together.

3. Slowly stretch up with the entire torso and arms as you push downward into lunge. Eventually your back heel should be flat on the floor.

Do 3 or 4 repetitions on each side.

For: Thighs and groin.

1. In a side lunge position with both feet flat on the floor, put one hand on your hip or out to the side.

2. Slowly bend from the waist until one elbow touches floor.

3. Then extend other arm straight up toward ceiling. Hold for a few seconds.

4. Repeat stretch on the other side.

Do 3 to 4 repetitions on each side.

BACK ARM STRETCH

Pre-Senior
Citizen
(Stretching)

FOR: Arms and shoulders.

1. Hands clasped behind back, place body in a lunge position, elbows locked and back heel up.

2. Bend over from the waist reaching arms up in back of you. Lift clasped hands as high as possible.

3. Hold in bent position for 3 to 5 seconds.

4. Raise body back up to start position.

5. Change legs so other one is in front and repeat stretch.

Do 3 to 4 repetitions on each leg.

FOR: Legs, hips, abdomen, torso, arms and shoulders.

1. Extend arms in front of you. Assume side lunge position.
2. Lock elbows, fists clenched to stress forearms and upper arms.
3. Slowly swing arms from side to side, twisting torso left and right as well. Be sure to put stress on forward bent leg.

Do 4 to 6 repetitions in each direction.

TORSO TWIST

Pre-Senior Citizen

GROIN AND THIGH STRETCH

Pre-Senior
Citizen
(Stretching)

FOR: Legs, ankles to thigh. Improves balance.

1. In a deep lunge position, back leg extended and up on toes, stretch downward until knee touches the floor.

2. Angle body back so you can touch extended leg with corresponding hand.

3. As you develop control of balance, bend extended leg up toward your body.

Repeat twice on each side.

NOTE: **Work to keep your balance and your back erect all during exercise.**

FOR: Ankles, up through buttocks, hips and back.

1. With feet comfortably apart, slowly bend knees as deeply as you are able, keeping your feet flat on the floor. Inhale as you bend down.

2. Hold the lowest position for a second or two.

3. Then, exhale as you slowly come up to a standing position.

Do 8 to 10 of these, arms extended.

NOTES:

1. **If need be, in the beginning, hold on to something stationary for support (such as kitchen counter, washbasin, etc.). Later, when you have progressed, do squats without extra support. To assist balance, some people may need to use an object under the heels (such as a phone book) until their flexibility increases.**

2. **Keep working at these squats until you can accomplish them standing flat on the floor.**

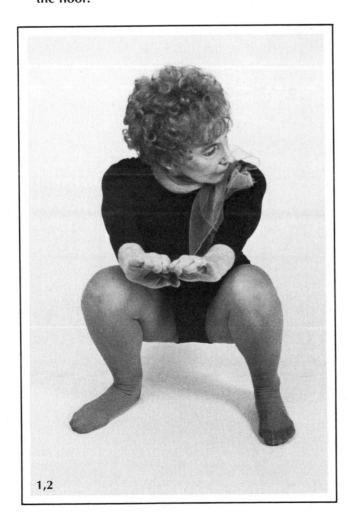

1,2

HAND ROTATION

Pre-Senior
Citizen
(Stretching)

FOR: Arms and shoulders.

With your arms bent directly in front of your chest, fingers straight, rotate the hands and forearms (motion originating at the elbow) slowly in one direction for 10 seconds, then reverse direction for 10 seconds.

Repeat rotations as rapidly as possible in both directions.

FOR: Arms and shoulders.

1. Start with one arm bent up over shoulder, other arm bent behind back. Bring the two hands together and clasp fingers.

2. Slowly bend high elbow down and over to the side.

3. Still holding fingers, turn hand till palm faces ceiling.

4. Continue bringing arm down, allowing elbow to bend in back of torso, still keeping fingers joined.

5. Slowly straighten out both elbows, hands clasped behind your back.

6. Do the same thing with the other arm bent up over your shoulder.

Do 1 time on each side.

NOTES:

1. **Doing this exercise as pictured here is dependent on your body structure and degree of flexibility. Find a way to modify it for yourself so you can get benefit from it.**

2. **Do *not* force the stretch.**

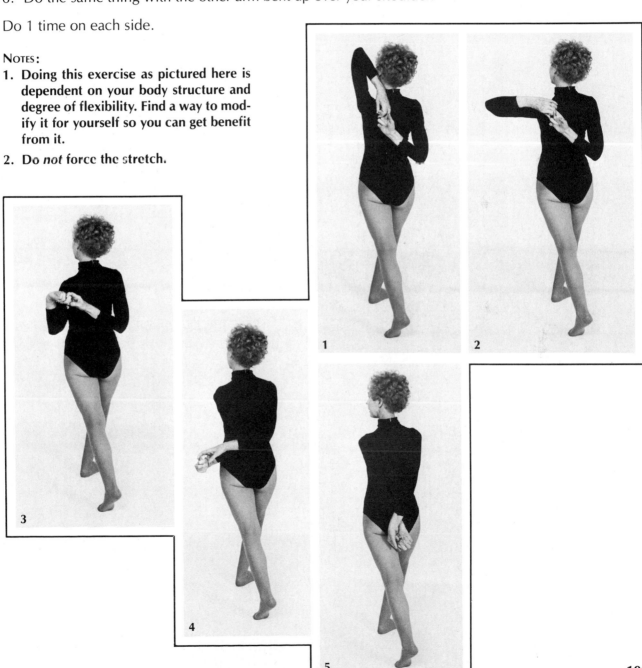

SEMI-SPLIT

Pre-Senior Citizen

FOR: Back, hips, thighs and groin.

1. Sitting on the floor, extend one leg forward while swinging the other leg behind you with your knee bent.

2. Slowly "walk" hands down the forward leg as far as you can toward your ankle and foot.

3. Bring head and torso as close to the forward leg as possible. When you reach this point, hold this position for 3 to 5 seconds.

4. Slowly walk your hands back up your leg to a sitting position. Reverse legs and repeat the above.

Do 2 to 3 repetitions on each side.

NOTE: **Do this very *slowly;* do not jar your body.**

FOR: Arms, shoulders, buttocks, hips, chest and abdomen. This is also especially beneficial for the lower back.

1. Kneel on the floor, assuming a catlike position with arms extended flat in front of you, supporting most of your body weight. Your torso should be tucked over your knees with the buttocks up.

2. Move torso forward, bending elbows and putting chin on floor, with buttocks raised.

3. From this position push chin through your arms in a *low,* forward sweeping movement, continuing the motion until legs are locked, elongated and flat along the floor. The motion continues by arching your back and slowly straightening your arms until the torso is nearly perpendicular to the body.

4. Using a fluid movement, slowly reverse the process until you have returned to the original catlike position.

Do 3 to 4 repetitions of this exercise *very, very slowly!*

CROSSOVER STRETCH

Pre-Senior Citizen

FOR: Waist, back of the thighs, buttocks.

1. Lie flat on floor, arms outstretched.
2. Raise right leg, keeping toes pointed, knees locked throughout exercise.
3. Slowly cross leg over body and reach toward opposite outstretched hand, touching it if possible. Slowly raise leg, then lower it back to start position.
4. Do same with other leg.

Do 3 to 4 repetitions on each side.

VARIATION:

1. Raise both legs, toes pointed and knees locked, both arms stretched out to your sides.
2. Slowly cross both legs over to one side toward outstretched hand.
3. Bring back to center position and cross legs to other side.
4. Bring legs back to center and down slowly with heels flexed.

Do 3 to 4 repetitions on each side.

For: Upper torso, midsection, hips, buttocks and thighs.

1. Lie in a prone position with your knees bent, feet flat on the floor, hands behind head.

2. Using neck muscles and arms, elevate your head.

3. Pull up one leg, touching knee to opposite elbow.

4. Repeat with the other leg.

Do 8 to 10 repetitions on each side.

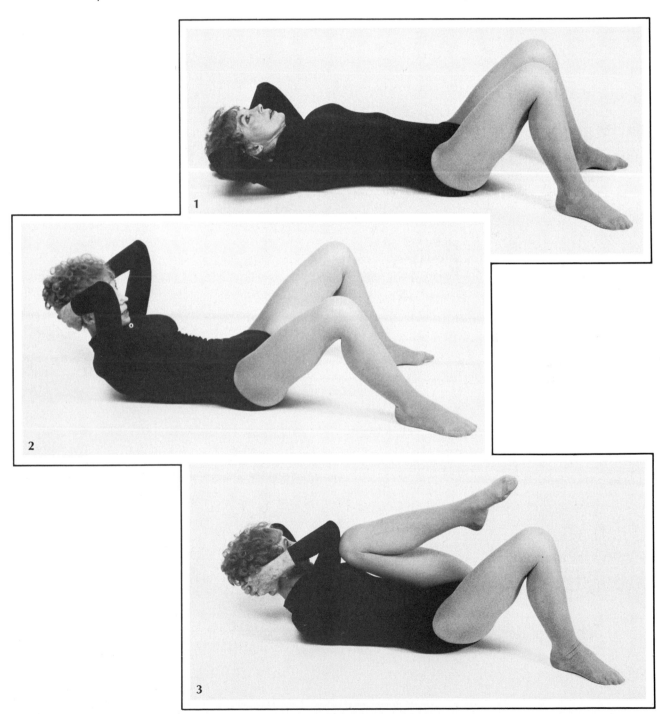

CROSSED-ARM ABDOMINAL STRETCH

Pre-Senior Citizen

For: Arms, back, abdomen and buttocks.

1. Lie in a prone position with knees bent and feet flat on the floor. Cross arms over the chest.
2. Inhale and hold breath.
3. Use stomach muscles to pull body into a sitting position or as high as you can get. Try *not* to use the small of the back.
4. Once you are in a sitting position, or as high as you can get, exhale and slowly, with control, lower the torso back to the original position.

Do 6 to 8 repetitions. Add more repetitions as you get stronger.

NOTE: **Do the entire sequence *very, very slowly,* both going up and down. The slower you do this exercise the more beneficial it is.**

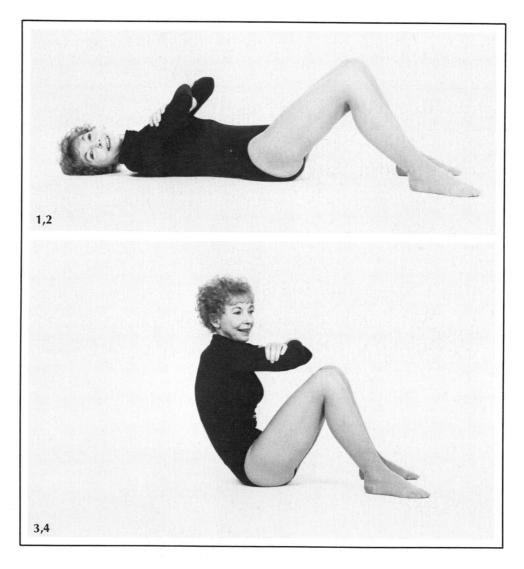

1,2

3,4

FOR: Legs, buttocks, hips and midsection.

1. Assume start position: shoulders firmly on the floor, back arched, knees bent and feet flat on the floor, thus forming a bridge. Use arms and hands to support buttocks and lower back.

2. Straighten legs out in front of you. Your weight should be resting on your head, shoulders, arms and feet.

3. Raise one leg, toes pointed. Balance, then raise second leg, toes pointed holding body almost vertical.

4. Pump legs in "bicycle pedaling" movement for at least 30 to 60 seconds— or to heart's content.

5. Slowly lower one leg, then the other, first to arch position and then to prone position.

NOTE: Try and do as much of the exercise as possible. Don't attempt the bicycle in this position until you're able to support yourself adequately. This one's going to take an awful lot of practice, but you'll benefit greatly as you are able to progress.

THE PLOW WITH A FEW EXTRAS

Pre-Senior Citizen

FOR: Suppleness of entire body.

An old, old yoga favorite, the plow is not all that difficult to do, but does require a degree of suppleness. It stretches the spine, as well as almost every other part of the body.

1. Start position is on your shoulders. Raise legs vertically with one arm supporting the body at the hips, the other extended out flat. If you need more support, put both hands at hips. Throughout exercise, work to stay up on your shoulders, keeping back straight, buttocks lifted. Eventually, entire body from shoulders to toes should form one line.

2. Bend knees and lower legs until the knees touch the forehead.

3. Extend legs and feet straight back, forming a V, parallel to the floor, until the toes touch the floor.

4. Hold the position for 3 to 5 seconds.

5. Then shift the legs to one side of the head and bend knees to the floor. Do the same on the other side.

6. Slowly reverse steps of exercise until you are back at start position. Then slowly lower back onto the floor, keeping legs straight. Lower legs across face and torso to stretch spine and bring yourself all the way down to prone position. You can use your arms to help you if necessary.

7. Rest for a moment; repeat whole process.

Do complete exercise 1 or 2 times.

FOR: Hips, buttocks, thighs, abdomen, waist.

1. Lie on your side supporting torso with one elbow and the other hand.
2. Slowly raise top leg, knee locked, toe pointed, until extended and stretched as high as possible.
3. Bring lower leg up to meet raised leg in midair. Lower both legs slowly.
4. Turn to opposite side and repeat exercise, other leg going up first.

Do 3 repetitions on each side.

VARIATION: Lift legs six inches off the floor and slowly swing top leg forward and bottom leg back simultaneously. Keep toes pointed and legs straight throughout exercise.

STOMACH STRETCH

Pre-Senior
Citizen

FOR: Upper torso, back, shoulders and midsection.

1. Lying on your stomach, extend arms forward.
2. Raise upper body and open arms to form a V, with palms on the floor.
3. Bring arms back and to your sides, keeping torso up off floor.
4. Raise arms and clasp hands behind your back. Hold this stretch position 3 to 5 seconds.
5. Slowly reverse process returning to start position.

Do 3 or 4 repetitions.

FOR: Abdomen, thighs and buttocks.

1. Lie on the floor on your stomach. Clasp hands behind back, knees locked with toes touching floor.

2. Lift upper body off the floor, arching up as high as you are able. Hold for 3 to 5 seconds.

3. Then lower body back to the floor.

Do torso lift 4 to 6 times.

4. Move hands from behind your back to under your pelvis.

5. Lift lower body off the floor, legs going as high as possible. Hold this position for 3 to 5 seconds.

6. Slowly lower legs to the start position.

Do leg lifts 3 to 5 times.

NOTE: **As with everything, a person must use caution. Don't jerk or jar, but slowly stretch only as far in either direction as your body will easily go. Breathe in whenever lifting a part of your body and exhale while letting that area down.**

TEETER-TOTTER STRETCH

Pre-Senior Citizen

1,2,3

4,5,6

ABDOMEN AND THIGHS

Pre-Senior Citizen

FOR: Thighs, groin, knees, stomach.

Supporting body with right hand, right leg extended fully, raise left leg and clasp at ankle. Slowly pull it toward your back. You'll feel the stretch all the way from the thigh to the chest. Switch sides and support body with left hand and pull on right leg.

Do 2 to 5 times on each leg.

FOR: Upper body: arms, back, waist; lower body: hips and thighs.

1. Start position: sitting on the edge of a chair with feet flat on floor, clasp hands above head. Stretch upward.

2. Retaining stretch, and keeping back as flat as possible, bend forward. Touch floor, then rise back to start position.

3. Stretch side to side as far as possible with hands clasped over head.

Do 6 repetitions each direction.

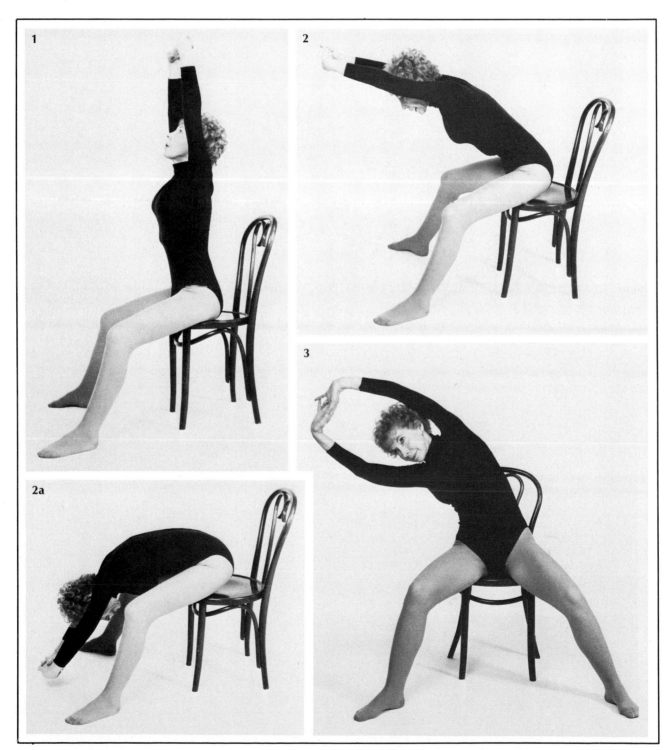

NO-ACHE FORWARD BACKBEND

Pre-Senior Citizen
(Chair)

FOR: Back and hip sockets.

1. Start position: sit forward on a chair. Slowly place hands on small of back keeping elbows back.
2. Bend body forward, slowly, as far as possible. Return to sitting position.

Do 10 repetitions.

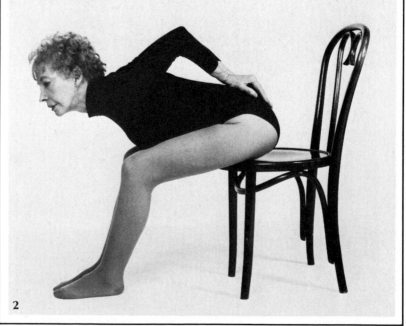

FOR: Thighs and legs.

1. Start position: sit on edge of chair and grasp front of chair.

2. Lift legs into bicycling position and begin pumping.

Pump away for 20 seconds, slowly building up to longer periods of time.

CHAIR LIFT

Pre-Senior
Citizen
(Chair)

FOR: Legs, thighs, abdomen, arms, shoulders. Super for firming up arms and
toning stomach muscles.

1. Start position: grasp side of chair and plant feet firmly on the floor.

2. Lift buttocks off the chair. Keep back straight.

Do 10 repetitions.

FOR: Arms, legs, shoulders.

This one is deceptive, not the easiest exercise in the book, but great for the entire body.

1. Start position: squat in front of a chair, feet firmly planted. With arms behind you, grasp edge of chair seat.

2. Lower buttocks till you are only an inch or two from the floor. Recover.

Do 5 repetitions.

NOTE: **Make sure chair is positioned against a wall for support so it—and you—won't move or fall backward.**

SEMI-LOTUS IN CHAIR

Pre-Senior
Citizen
(Chair)

FOR: Thighs and groin.

This one is a true test of flexibility.

1. Sit well back in chair. Using your arms as support, raise either right or left leg.

2. Twist leg and knee out to the side as far as possible, bringing toe slightly over opposite leg.

Do 3 repetitions on each leg.

NOTE: **Remember, you must slowly build up your flexibility!**

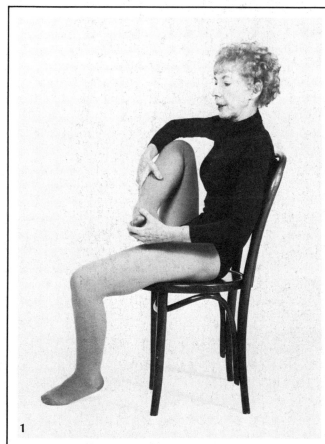

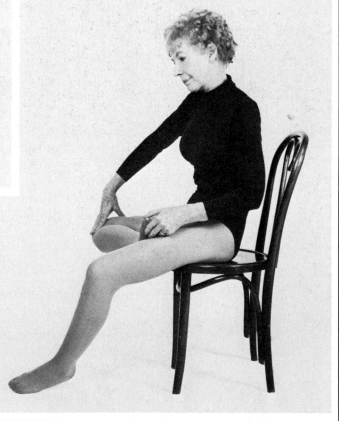

FOR: Thighs, hips, waistline, midsection.

1. Sitting in a chair, cross your left leg over your right, then turn your torso to the left, grasping seat of chair to increase the twist a bit.

2. Then, to increase twist further, cross right leg over left.

3. Perform exercise again, this time with right leg over left at the start.

Do 8 twists—4 each direction.

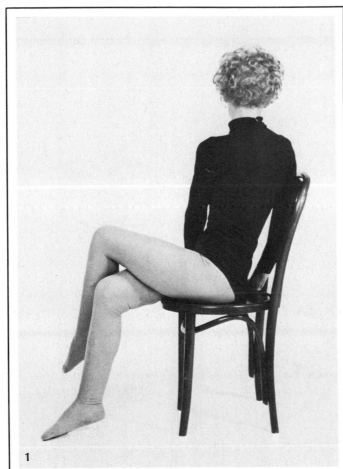

ROTATION PARTNERS

Pre-Senior
Citizen

FOR: Pulls torso, stretches crotch and tightens buttocks.

1. Partners face each other on the floor, spreading legs wide apart and touching feet or ankles and grasping hands.

2. With one partner acting as "anchor," the other partner leans forward as far as possible, then to the side as far as possible, then back around in a circle—head almost touching floor—to the other side and then coming back up to the start position.

Do 5 rotations and then switch roles and repeat.

NOTE: **This exercise benefits both partners, for each person stretches the different parts of the body throughout the exercise.**

FOR: Legs, groin, abdomen, rib cage, shoulders and arms.

1. Seated on floor facing each other, partners put feet or ankles together to form a diamond shape and clasp hands.

2. Alternately pull and lean back. Each partner touches head to floor in a seesaw motion. Do it *slowly* and *gently*.

3. Return to start position. Slowly lean to one side, with arms held high, stretching the inner arms as well as the shoulders, neck, groin and buttocks. Stretch arms overhead on the floor.

4. Then, return to start position and slowly lean to the other side.

Do entire exercise 6 times.

NOTE: Be sure to not force the stretching. Move slowly and gently throughout the exercise.

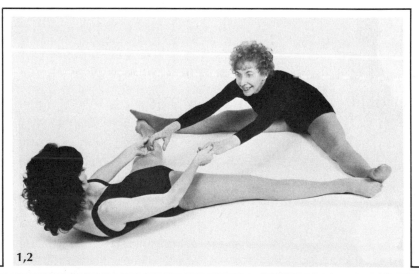

1,2

3

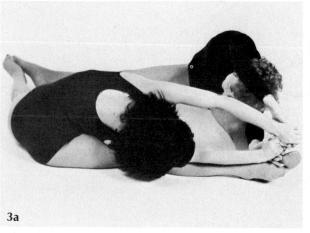

3a

STRAIGHT LEG SEESAW

Pre-Senior Citizen

FOR: Torso, feet to buttocks to shoulders.

1. Sit on floor, placing soles of feet together, with knees locked, hands clasped.

2. Slowly seesaw back and forth.

Do 10 repetitions.

NOTE: **Movements should be slow and gentle, not short and choppy.**

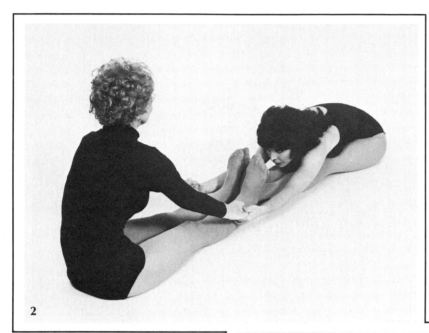

FOR: Inner thigh and groin.

1. One partner lies on side, propped up by arms. Other partner, the "resister," kneels, placing slight weight on partner's leg.

2. First partner lifts leg 6 to 12 inches, working against resister's force.

Do 6 to 8 repetitions with each leg, then change legs. Then change positions.

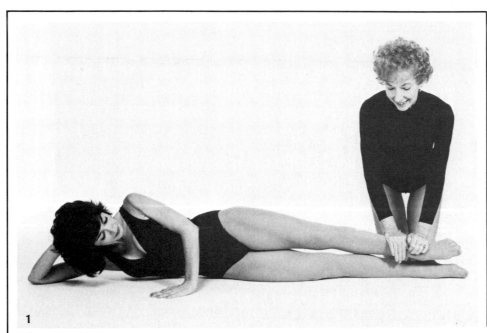

HORSE

Pre-Senior
Citizen

FOR: Shoulders, neck and arms of the "horse"; thighs, arms and abdomen for "rider."

1. The "horse" is prone; "rider" sits just above the knee area. Horse's arms are extended behind, with rider grasping at the wrists.

2. Rider pulls back as far as each person can stretch.

Do 6 to 8 repetitions. Then switch places.

1

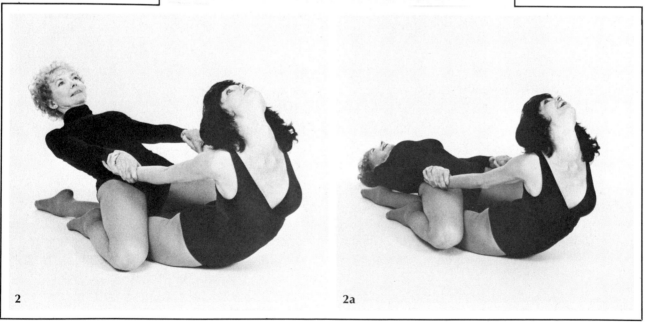

2   2a

214

17

SENIOR CITIZEN

God and medical science willing, I'll someday be a senior citizen and only hope that I can stay in shape up to that time and during it. I've seen too many seniors on running ground and in gyms to be the least bit sympathetic when I'm told, "Oh, I can't do that. I'm turning seventy-six." So what! Seniors should be respected for activity, not inactivity.

If pre-senior citizens can pick and choose from *all* the exercises, then seniors have even more right to try anything in this book—*in any way they want. Adaptation* is the key here, I believe. If the exercise works better seated in a chair, so be it. If the stretch is helped by doing it in the swimming pool, terrific! If you want to adapt a whole routine of stretches for performing in the bed, super! What I'd like to stress most is that a conditioning program can be started at any age, definitely including the eighties and nineties. If I were in charge of a retirement home, I'd hang stretching illustrations in every bathroom; I'd put a pair of 2-pound dumbbells beside every bed. Seniors, more than any other age category, need to have muscles stretched and pain pockets eliminated.

WHEN?   Whenever you please.

HOW?   See the following pages, plus any other exercise in the book that looks interesting.

TIPS 1. Adapt whatever exercise you'd like to do to your own circumstances.

2. Do not place yourself in any danger while doing the exercises. Do not attempt those that might cause you to fall or injure muscles.

3. *Go slowly.* Time should not be a factor.

4. Many of the stretching exercises can be accomplished in a bed as well as on the floor. Simply adapt them.

5. Lifting light weights is a valid, helpful exercise for a 90-year-old, providing that person *has the strength to lift and control them.*

Long ago I was impressed with Larry Lewis, the 100-plus-year-old running waiter in San Francisco. I'm equally impressed with the model for this section—92-year-old Leo Kachadourian, retired dentist and wellness/fitness devotee.

FOR: Arms and shoulders.

1. Alternately raise and lower arms, reaching back as far as possible.

Do 20 to 25 repetitions on each arm.

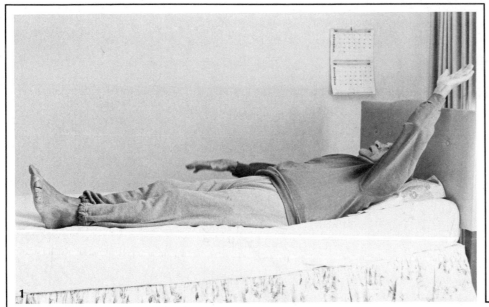

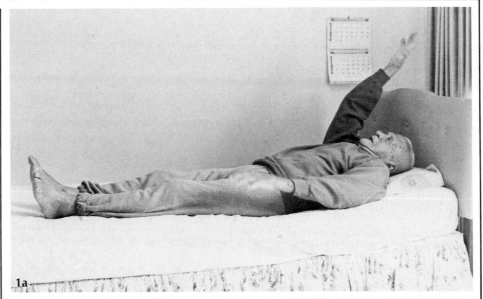

FINGER FLEX

Senior Citizen

FOR: Fingers and hands.

1. Begin at a position with hands clasped over the waist.
2. Move arms upward until they are fully extended, flexing (opening and closing) hands all the way up. Flex fingers for 10 to 20 seconds and then slowly bring arms down—still flexing.

Raise and lower arms 5 times, concentrating on increasing movement in your hands.

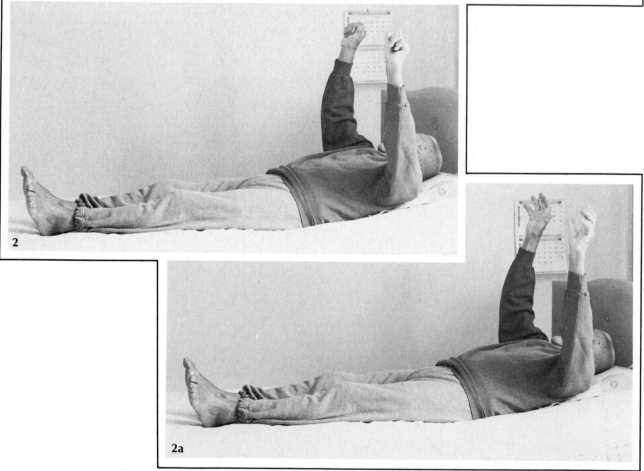

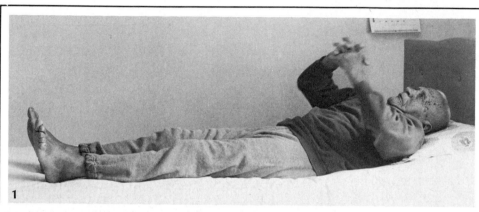

For: Thighs, abdomen, calves, hips, toes.

The bed is a fine platform for vigorous leg exercises.

1. From a prone position, extend legs, stretching the muscles to the fullest.
2. Flexing the feet and using the hands to support the leg, extend the leg up, perpendicular to your body. As you lift the leg, make sure you point and flex the foot.

Do 5 repetitions on each leg.

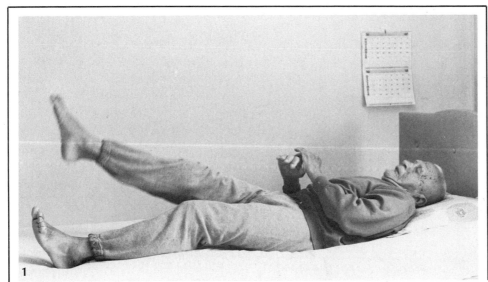

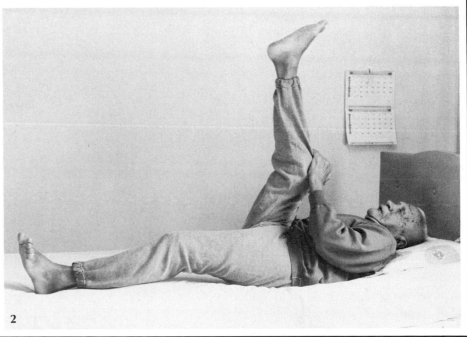

KNEE FLEXES

Senior
Citizen

FOR: Groin, knees, thighs, hips, buttocks, abdomen.

Keeping the knees flexible is very important for older people, who tend to become less active with age.

1. From a prone position, bend the knees toward the chest, controlling the degree of the stretch with the hands. Alternate.

Do 10 repetitions, 5 with each leg.

2. Put feet together—sole to sole—and apply gentle, slow, steady pressure on the knees to open them as far as possible.

Do 4 to 6 repetitions.

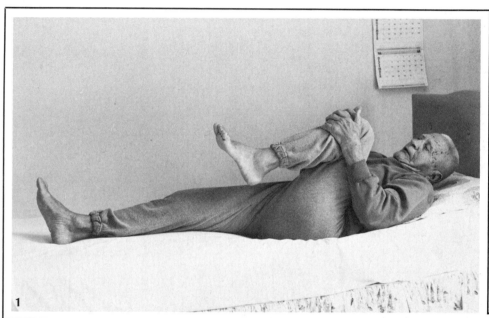

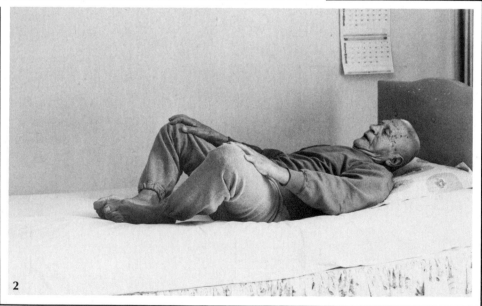

FOR: Back, thighs, buttocks, shoulders and arms.

On hands and knees, stretch like a cat. Start with buttocks up and head down—bring torso forward and reach up with head and neck.

Do 4 or 5 repetitions (slowly).

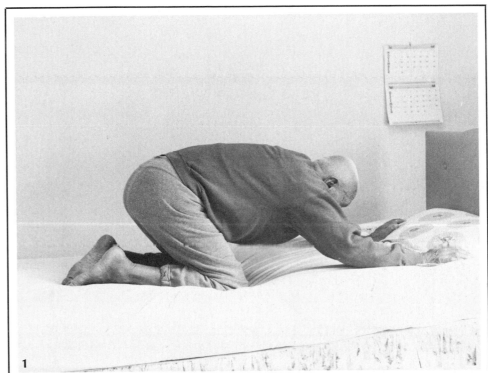

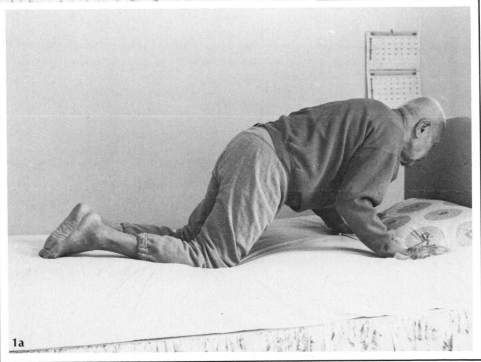

CHANGE OF PACE

Senior
Citizen

FOR: Blood flow, arms, shoulders, calves.

All bed exercises don't have to be accomplished on top of the bed. Try half on, half off.

1. Lower body remains on the bed; bend the upper body over the side of the bed toward the floor over a carpet, rubber padding or mat.
2. Using head, arms and shoulders as support, kick your feet vigorously.

Do 30 seconds to one minute, but do it as long as you like.

VARIATION: Stand on your head with no arm support. You can use a pillow for comfort, if you want to.

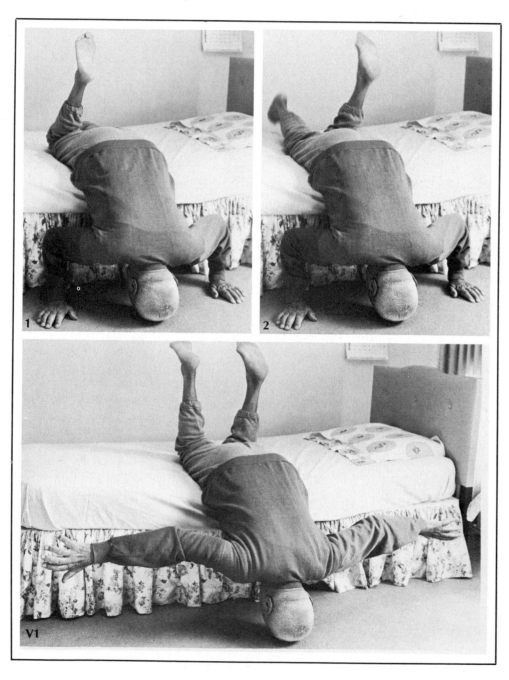

CARDIO-
VASCULAR AND
STRETCHING
EXERCISES

Senior
Citizen

FOR: Arms, shoulders, back, thighs, calves.

Swimming, of course, is a super cardiovascular exercise for all ages, but a pool offers possibilities for stretching, particularly for senior citizens who have difficulty with balance and control or other problems. The water provides support for the body while exercising.

A. Holding on to the assist rails at the walk-up, lean back into the water then pull up using arms and shoulders; calves, thighs, back muscles. Do 10 repetitions.

B. Muscle resistance with light weights. Place shoulder blades against pool side. Using light dumbbells in each hand, thrust your arms out, beneath the surface of the water. Benefits arms and shoulders. Do 20 repetitions alternating (10 for each side).

C. With back against pool side, bend knees in and extend legs in slow stretches. Do 20 repetitions alternating (10 for each side).

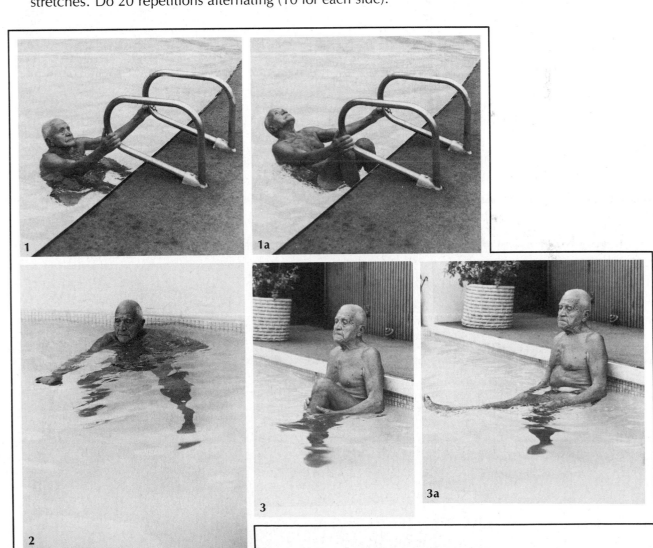

WALL REACH

Senior Citizen

FOR: Arms and shoulders.

Reach as high as you can up the wall with one arm, extending the other arm toward the floor as far as possible. You'll feel the pull beneath the extended arm, stretching all the way down the rib cage. Alternating arms, do 4 to 5 reaches with each arm—*slowly!*

NOTE: If your arm doesn't go high on the wall, don't worry about it. Gradually, it will. Let your hand and fingers "walk" up the wall—each workout go a little higher. Before you know it, your arms will be over your head straight (and you'll lift them without the support of the wall!).

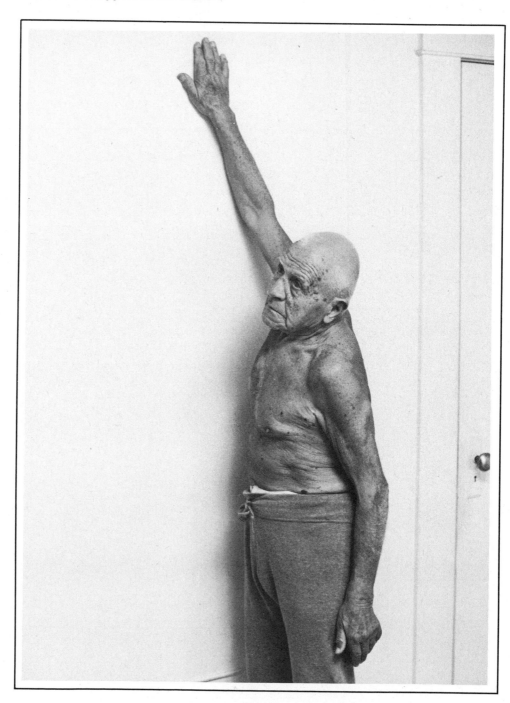

FOR: Arms, shoulder, abdomen, legs, calves.

This exercise isn't worth a good hosanna unless you come off your heels and reach for the sky with your arms raised, feeling every muscle pulling.

Do 5 to 6 repetitions.

NOTE: **Keep back flush up against the wall for support.**

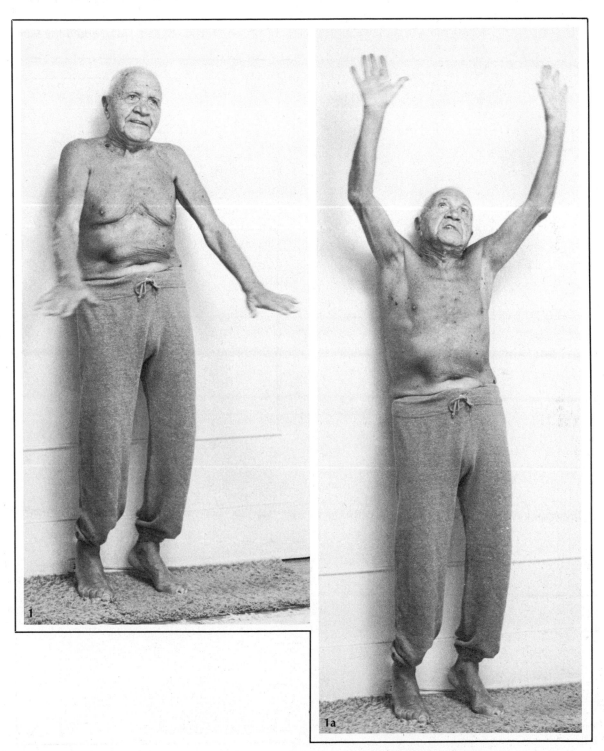

WASHBASIN BALLET

Senior
Citizen

The washbasin serves as a fine, steady platform for bathroom exercises—before or after brushing the teeth, perhaps. Of course, other sturdy supports are fine.

1. Using the sink for resistance, pull upward against it. You'll feel the muscles in your legs and back working. Good!

2. Use the sink as an anchor to squat as low as possible. You'll feel the muscles in your shoulders and back stretching.

3. Turn around and use the basin as an anchor to do forward bends, keeping the feet planted.

4. Use the basin as a support to perform back stretches.

Do 10 repetitions of each.

FOR: Pulls and stretches arms, thighs, calves.

1. Starting in a prone position, cross your legs and grasp toes.
2. Roll backward.

Do as many as you like.

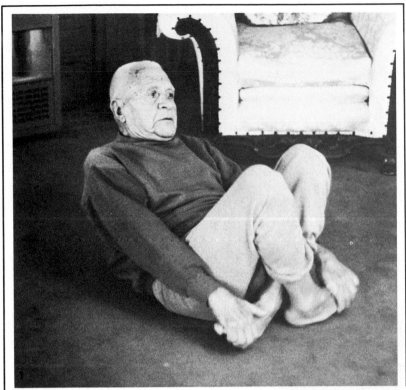

AIR SWEEP

Senior Citizen

FOR: Arms, shoulders, rib cage, obliques (sides of waist), abdomen.

Swing broom (or other not-too-heavy, long pole) in both directions, 25 repetitions, resting when necessary.

FOR: Arms, back and legs.

Throw a length of rope about 8 feet long around any stationary object for support. Either sway from side to side or jump, feet opening and closing.

Do 10 to 12 repetitions. Rest a minute, then do 10 to 12 repetitions. Rest for another minute, then maybe do a third set of 10 to 12 repetitions.

TOMATO CAN LIFTS

Senior
Citizen

FOR: Arms and shoulders.

If you don't have light weights (2½ to 5 pounds) around the house, try a pair of tomato cans weighing 1 pound, 12 ounces or heavier.

1. Start with cans in front of you.

2. Lift them out to the side and up.

Do 5 to 6 repetitions.

18

SUGGESTED ROUTINES

The following sets of routines are suggestions *only*—springboards from which to create your own workout in order to focus on the specific areas you need.

The Monday-Wednesday-Friday workouts include stretching and weight lifting within the half hour and hour time frame. The Tuesday-Thursday-Saturday-Sunday workout stretches are in addition to the half hour or full hour exercises.

After you are acclimated to these exercises, you will notice that it takes less time to accomplish them fully. You will shorten your workout by at least 10 minutes.

Remember—you can substitute your own choice of exercises. Enjoy!

Mon • Wed • Fri
STRETCHING
and
WEIGHT LIFTING
PROGRAM

One half hour
for beginners

STRETCHING

1. Good-Morning Stretch: p. 80
2. Arm Circles: p. 83
3. Knee Lift Balance: p. 72
4. Forward Lunge (Bent Leg): p. 75
5. Full-Circle Reach: p. 88

6. Oblique Stretch: p. 92
7. Flexed Foot Stretch: p. 99
8. One-Leg Reach Over: p. 117
9. Scissor Stretch: p. 116

If you have time, add other suitable exercises.

WEIGHTS:

1. Clean and Press, p. 140: start with very low weight—even if you feel you can handle more—until your muscles adapt to the lifting form. Do 3 sets, starting with 6 repetitions and decreasing repetitions as you add more weight.

   EXAMPLE: *First set*—bar with collars or 5-pound weights on each side (do 6 to 8 repetitions clean and press).

   Second set—bar with 10- or 15-pound weights on each side (do 4 to 6 repetitions clean and press).

   Third set—bar with 15 to 20-pound weights on each side (do 3 to 4 repetitions clean and press).

   NOTE:
   For those who have never before had the opportunity to lift weights or do this particular exercise, I suggest you stay with the same amount of weight used for the first set and the same number of repetitions until you feel secure enough to increase the weights.

2. Behind Neck Press, p. 144 or 145 (sitting or standing): again use minimal amount of weight.

   EXAMPLE: Do 1 set (6 to 8 repetitions) with bar and collars, or if you can handle weight, 5 to 10 pounds on each side.

3. Squat, p. 146 or 148 (front or back): again using minimal amount of weight until your body is acclimated to the form.

   EXAMPLE: Do 1 set (6 to 8 repetitions) using bar with collars, or 10 to 15 pounds on each side.

4. Fly, p. 135: Lying on a bench do 6 repetitions slowly in each direction (in other words, 24 total repetitions).

NOTE:
Use your discretion, listen to your body *(don't force)* and when you know it's telling you, "I'm capable of doing more," then and *only* then extend yourself by adding more weights and repetitions if need be.

Also, after each set of weights, do the Good-Morning Stretch (2 repetitions on each side). Then rest 2 to 3 minutes before going on to the next set of weights. If you need more time to rest between any exercise, take it, don't overtax yourself in your beginning stages.

1. Good-Morning Stretch: p. 80
2. Assorted Stretches: p. 158
3. Either start with basic suggestions in Chapter Seven or walk, run or jog for 10, 20 or 30 minutes.

(Do the same on all of the above days)

NOTE: Other suggestions on your cardiovascular days are to either jump rope, bike or swim (a good substitute on a trip or during inclement weather is a jump rope).

End of run:
1. Runner's Stretches: p. 157
2. Overall Stretch and Relaxer: p. 156
   Walk around until your body cools down and pulse rate is back close to normal.

Same exercises each day:

1. Good-Morning Stretch: p. 80
2. Head Roll: p. 81
3. Arm Circles: p. 83
4. Knee Lift Balance: p. 72
5. Forward Reach: p. 87
6. Half-Circle Reach: p. 89
7. Forward Lunge (Bent Leg): p. 75
8. Full-Circle Reach: p. 88
9. Flat-Footed Half Squat: p. 86
10. Oblique Stretch: p. 92
11. Lunge Stretch: Elbow Touch: p. 185
12. "Growing Tree" Stretch: p. 77
13. Wraparound Stretch: p. 98
14. Seated Reach: p. 100
15. Flexed Foot Stretch: p. 99
16. One-Leg Reach Over: p. 117
17. Scissor Stretch: p. 116
18. Ski Turn: p. 95
19. Around the World: p. 120

Mon • Wed • Fri STRETCHING and WEIGHT LIFTING PROGRAM

NOTE: Use your discretion, listen to your body and don't rush or force—only extend yourself when you really know you're ready and able to. Also, after each set of weights, do the Good-Morning Stretch, 2 repetitions on each side and rest 2 to 3 minutes before going on to next set.

WEIGHTS:

1. Clean and Press, p. 140: start with very low weights—even if you feel you can handle more—until your muscles adapt to the lifting form. Do 3 sets starting with 6 repetitions and decreasing.

   EXAMPLE: *First set*—bar with collars or 5-pound weights on each side (do 6 to 8 repetitions clean and press).

   Second set—bar with 10- or 15-pound weights on each side (do 4 to 6 repetitions clean and press).

   Third set—bar with 15- to 20-pound weights on each side (do 3 or 4 repetitions clean and press).

NOTE: **For those who have never before had the opportunity to lift weights or do this particular exercise, I suggest you stay with same amount of weight used for the first set and the same amount of repetitions until you feel secure enough to increase weights accordingly.**

2. Behind Neck Press, p. 144 or 145 (sitting or standing): again use minimal amount of weight.

   EXAMPLE: *First set*—6 to 8 repetitions with bar and collars or if you can, put 5 to 10 pounds on each side.

   Second set—4 to 5 repetitions with either 2½, 5 or 10 pounds added to each side of bar.

3. Squats, p. 147 or 149 (front or back on phone book): again using minimal amount of weight until your body is acclimated to the form.

   EXAMPLE: *First set*—6 to 8 repetitions using bar with collars or 10 to 15 pounds on each side.

   Second set—either same as above or, if you're able, increase the weight accordingly.

4. Upright Rowing Motion, p. 143: again use minimal amount of weight (6 to 8 repetitions).

   EXAMPLE: Bar with or without collars or 2½ to 5 pounds each side.

5. Flys, p. 135, or Straight Arm Standing Flys, p. 129: do 6 repetitions slowly in each direction (total of 24 repetitions).

Do same as half hour beginner (cardiovascular workout) except if you're able and up to it, extend your walk, run, biking, or add a few minutes of squat jumps or rope skipping plus any additional stretching (select one suitable to your needs). This will only support your getting into the shape you want sooner (or certainly support your progress).

1. Good-Morning Stretch: p. 80
2. Oblique Stretch: p. 92
3. Knee Lift Balance: p. 72
4. Forward Reach: p. 87
5. Half-Circle Reach: p. 89
6. Full-Circle Reach: p. 88
7. Jackknife Stretch: p. 90
8. Wall Knee Lifts: p. 94
9. Lateral Split Stretch I: p. 101
10. Scissor Stretch: p. 116
11. Standing Backbend: p. 93
12. Good-Morning Stretch: p. 80

If you have time, add other suitable exercises.

WEIGHTS:

1. Clean and Press: p. 140
2. Behind Neck Press (on bench or standing): p. 144 or 145
3. Straight Arm or Bent Arm Pullovers: p. 150 or p. 134
4. Straight Arm Flys (on bench or standing): p. 135 or 129

Tues • Thurs • Sat • Sun CARDIO-VASCULAR PROGRAM

Mon • Wed • Fri STRETCHING and WEIGHT LIFTING PROGRAM

Half Hour
Advanced
Program

Let's say that you've been jogging or running for a while now. Since you've chosen a half hour cardiovascular day, I assume you don't have that much time to spend because of work, household duties, or whatever, so besides the few stretch exercises you'll be doing before running, you'll still have time to run a minimum of at least 2 to 3 miles, which is more than adequate.

On days with inclement weather or trips away from home where you are not able to run, I suggest you bring along a jump rope or do squat jumps at home or in your hotel room.

STRETCHES BEFORE RUNNING:

1. Good-Morning Stretch: p. 80
2. Assorted Stretches: p. 158
3. Hamstring Stretch: p. 159

AFTER RUNNING:

Walk down pole or meter (p. 156) or hang onto something in bent-over squat position with arms extended (such as car fender or door).

NOTE: **This exercise is an excellent way of taking the stress off of upper and lower back after your run.**

Same exercises each day:

Mon • Wed • Fri
STRETCHING and
WEIGHT LIFTING
PROGRAM

One Hour
Advanced
Program

1. Good-Morning Stretch: p. 80
2. Basic Balance: p. 71
3. Upper Torso Isolation: p. 85
4. Standing Backbend: p. 93
5. Yoga Stretch Sequence: p. 106
6. Lotus Front and Back Stretch: p. 108
7. Leg Extensions (Lying Down): p. 125
8. Lateral Split Stretch I: p. 101
9. One-Leg Reach Over: p. 117
10. Around the World: p. 120
11. Scissor Stretch: p. 116
12. Plow with Variations: p. 110
13. Frog Stretch: p. 118
14. Hip Flex: p. 119
15. Leg Lift (Back): p. 126
16. Leg Lift (Front to Back): p. 124
17. Leg Lift (Side): p. 123
18. Side Pull-Ups I: p. 114
19. Ski Turn: p. 95
20. Good-Morning Stretch: p. 80

WEIGHTS:

1. Clean and Press, p. 140: 2 to 3 sets
2. Behind Neck Press, p. 145: 1 set
3. Squats (Behind Neck or Front Squat with phone book), p. 147 or 149: 1 set
4. Upright Rowing Motion, p. 143: 1 set
5. Bent Arm Pullovers, p. 134, or Straight Arm Pullovers, p. 150: 1 set
6. Flys (Straight Arm), p. 135: 1 set

Tues • Thur • Sat • Sun CARDIOVASCULAR PROGRAM

Advanced
1 hour program

1. Good-Morning Stretch: p. 80

2. Runner's Stretches: p. 157

3. Assorted Stretches: p. 158

4. Hamstring Stretch: p. 159

Now since we've got time (and it may not be all four days, which is all right), we can indulge a more extensive workout without the pressure of time being a factor (I personally find Saturday and Sunday a time to increase my cardiovascular workout).

Here we can do a minimum of 3 to 5 miles and then at least 4 to 6 sprints or more (something I find necessary for myself after a run). Finally I walk around for 3 to 5 minutes to cool down.

EXAMPLE: I start a slow jog for 5 to 10 yards, increase to half or three-quarter speed for another 5 to 10 yards. I'll do at least 4 to 6 and sometimes 8 sprints after a run—then walk around for about 5 minutes. I end by doing any number of stretches on the ground such as a plow and mid-section twist on ground.

The very last thing I do before getting into my car is to walk down pole stretch for the back.

ABOUT THE AUTHOR
A native of Auburn, New York, *Tony Cacciotti* began his career in New York City as an exercise instructor and professional performer. Combining these two roles in Los Angeles, he's helped many stars get in shape for their movies as well as coordinated stunts for different films. With Valerie Harper, Tony has formed TAL Productions and has several film projects planned for the future. Tony lives in Los Angeles.